Life Cycle
Theory
and
Pastoral Care

THEOLOGY AND PASTORAL CARE SERIES

edited by
Don S. Browning

Life Cycle Theory and Pastoral Care
 by Donald Capps

Religious Ethics and Pastoral Care
 by Don S. Browning

A Roman Catholic Theology of Pastoral Care
 by Regis A. Duffy, O.F.M.

DONALD CAPPS

Life Cycle Theory and Pastoral Care

Don S. Browning, *editor*

THEOLOGY AND PASTORAL CARE

FORTRESS PRESS

PHILADELPHIA

Library of Congress Cataloging in Publication Data

Capps, Donald.
  Life cycle theory and pastoral care.

  (Theology and pastoral care series)
  Includes bibliographical references.
  1. Pastoral psychology. 2. Pastoral theology.
3. Life cycle, Human. 4. Erikson, Erik H. (Erik
Homburger), 1902– . 5. Bible. O.T. Proverbs—
Criticism, interpretation, etc. I. Title. II. Series.
BV4012.C316 1983   253.5   83–5585
ISBN 0–8006–1726–6

K114C83   Printed in the United States of America   1–1726

To Walter, Roger, and Douglas
Prov. 23:24–25

Contents

Series Foreword

Our purpose in the Theology and Pastoral Care Series is to present ministers and church leaders with a series of readable books that will (1) retrieve the theological and ethical foundations of the Judeo-Christian tradition for pastoral care, (2) develop lines of communication between pastoral theology and the other disciplines of theology, (3) create an ecumenical dialogue on pastoral care, and (4) do this in such a way as to affirm, yet go beyond, the recent preoccupation of pastoral care with secular psychotherapy and the other social sciences.

The books in this series are written by authors who are well acquainted with psychology, psychotherapy, and the other social sciences. All of the authors affirm the importance of these disciplines for modern societies and for ministry in particular, but they see them also as potentially destructive of human values unless they are guided in their practical application by tested religious and ethical traditions. But to retrieve the best of the Judeo-Christian tradition for the church's care and counseling is a challenging intellectual task—a task to which few writers in the area of pastoral care have attended with sufficient thoroughness. This series addresses that task out of a broad ecumenical stance, with all of the authors taking an ecumenical approach to theology. Besides a vigorous investigation of Protestant resources, there are specific treatments of pastoral care in Judaism and Catholicism.

We hope that the series will help ministers and church leaders view afresh the theological and ethical foundations of care and counseling. All of the books have a practical dimension, but even more important than that, they help us see care and counseling differently. Compared with writings of the last thirty years in this field, some of the books will seem startlingly different. They will need to be read and pondered with care. But I have little doubt that the series will make a profound and lasting impact upon the way we understand and practice our care for one another.

Donald Capps, the author of this volume, is a young man who already has made outstanding contributions to the areas of both pastoral theology and the psychology of religion. After a wide and varied teaching career at Oregon State University, the University of Chicago, the University of North Carolina at Charlotte, and the Graduate Seminary at Phillips University, he is now Professor of Pastoral Theology at Princeton Theological Seminary. He is also the author of a significant number of books and articles in both pastoral care and the psychology of religion, his most widely known book being *Pastoral Care: A Thematic Approach*. More recently, he has authored *Pastoral Counseling and Preaching* and *Biblical Approaches to Pastoral Counseling*.

In *Life Cycle Theory and Pastoral Care* Don brings his considerable theological talents and his intimate knowledge of the psychology of Erik Erikson to bear on the challenge of giving pastoral order to the milestones and crises of the human life cycle. In addition to providing one of the clearest introductions available to the psychology of Erikson, he presents sparklingly original chapters on the problem of shame (which begins in early childhood but frequently lingers throughout life) and the task of achieving wisdom during the last stages of life. He offers creative new understandings of the traditional "deadly vices" and relates them to specific tasks and temptations which emerge at different points in the human life cycle. And finally, in a highly suggestive way, he demonstrates certain affinities between Erikson and the values and sensibilities of the wisdom tradition in the Scriptures of both the Old and the New Testaments.

Don offers two significantly new images of the pastor that will go far toward enriching our understanding of the care of the church—the minister as moral counselor and the minister as ritual coordinator. And he calls for renewed attention to a third traditional image—the minister as personal comforter. With these three images, Don enables us to understand the task of pastoral care as that of providing consistent patterns for living which help us to stabilize our needs and passions, channel our anxieties and anger, find predictable absolution for our guilt, and establish consistent sources of renewal and joy. In this fine book pastoral care becomes not only the response of the church to moments of crisis but also a way of shaping the lives of Christians between crises. Pastoral care becomes a method for helping Christians to live and renew their lives together.

DON S. BROWNING

Preface

There are two ways to use developmental theory in pastoral care. One is to better understand the various age groups to which we minister. Books that take this approach focus on selected age groups or on critical periods in life, such as the currently popular "mid-life crisis." The second is to better understand the nature and purpose of pastoral care. In books of this second type concepts of selected developmental theories are used to clarify the purposes and goals of pastoral care. The first approach focuses on the recipients of pastoral care, the second on those who do the caring.

I take the second approach here. I use Erik Erikson's developmental theory to clarify the purposes and goals of pastoral care. Erikson's theory of the life cycle directs our attention to issues we might otherwise not take seriously enough, issues that are critical in clarifying the purposes and goals of pastoral care. In an earlier book, *Pastoral Care: A Thematic Approach,*[1] I used Erikson's life cycle theory to draw attention to one such issue—the role of pastoral care in personal and institutional change. In this book I take up another important and parallel issue—the role of pastoral care in helping persons become better oriented in their world.

The topics discussed here focus around this vital issue. After the introductory chapter, which describes Erikson's life cycle theory, each chapter takes up a topic that centers on the fact that pastoral care has a fundamental responsibility for assisting people in becoming better oriented in the world.

Chapters 2—4 discuss three major roles of the pastor (moral counselor, ritual coordinator, and personal comforter) as pastoral responses to three major threats to our being oriented in the world.

Chapter 2 concerns the role of moral counselor; it takes up the disorienting factor of moral confusion and explores the role of the "deadly vices" in creating such confusion. Chapter 3 concerns the role of ritual coordinator; it addresses the need for a life that is meaningful and comprehensible and develops the thesis that this need is addressed through the ritualization of everyday church life. Chapter 4 concerns the role of personal comforter; it addresses the disorienting effects of severe pain and treats shame as a paradigmatic instance of disorienting pain. These three chapters employ Erikson's life cycle theory to show that a major function of pastoral care is to help persons become better oriented in their world.

Chapter 5 develops this view into a new pastoral care model. This model, which I call the model of "therapeutic wisdom," embraces the pastoral roles of moral counselor, ritual coordinator, and personal comforter. To formulate this model I explore the connections between Erikson's life cycle theory and the wisdom tradition of ancient Israel, especially as represented in the Book of Proverbs.

In dealing with the implications of Erikson's life cycle theory for pastoral care, my earlier book gave more attention to pastoral counseling issues. The present book focuses more on the moral, social, and institutional contexts in which pastoral care occurs. I owe my emphasis on the pastor as moral counselor in no small measure to Don Browning's *The Moral Context of Pastoral Care*.[2] The present book is also more concerned than the earlier one with providing a biblical foundation for pastoral care and thus continues some directions I staked out in my *Biblical Approaches to Pastoral Counseling*.[3] An emphasis found here, as in *Pastoral Care: A Thematic Approach*, is on the issue of the pastoral care of the church. My discussion of the everyday ritualization of the church in chapter 3 expands on chapters in the earlier book that dealt with psychosocial themes in the local church, and the thematic dimensions of institutional crisis. But the major connection between these two books is that together they focus on what I consider the two most fundamental issues in pastoral care—helping people toward positive change and enabling them to become better oriented in the world. If we reject the erroneous idea that such orientation is mere adjustment to the world, then these two functions of pastoral care can be seen as quite complementary, not antithetical. Thus the two books, the first with its emphasis on change and the present one with its stress on orientation to the world, go together.

I am grateful to Don Browning for his valuable comments on an earlier draft of this book. I thank James Butler for directing me to writings on the theme of wisdom literature and pastoral ministry, discussed in chapter 5. My appreciation is expressed also to Michael McKay and Laurel Ragland for insightful seminar papers on topics treated in this book. I am especially grateful to Erik Erikson for graciously consenting to talk with me at length about his life cycle theory and understandings of religion. This conversation, which took place 18 December 1981 at his home in Tiburon, California, has contributed enormously to setting the course I have taken in this book.

CHAPTER 1

Erikson's
Life Cycle
Theory

Erik Erikson's life cycle theory was first presented in his *Childhood and Society,* published in 1950. It was here, in a chapter entitled "Eight Ages of Man," that he laid out the eight psychosocial stages which have become the hallmark of his work as a developmental theorist. He applied this stage theory in his study of the early life of Martin Luther in 1958 and discussed its implications for a psychological view of "the healthy personality" in 1959.[1] Five years later Erikson provided a moral foundation for his stages by proposing a corresponding "schedule of virtues,"[2] and two years after that he proposed eight "stages in the ritualization of human experience."[3] Erikson's life cycle theory can be approached in various ways, but I like to think of it as having three major elements: the eight psychosocial stages, the schedule of virtues, and the stages in the ritualization of human experience.

I will be concerned in this chapter with the psychosocial stages, focusing primarily on the basic framework formulated in 1950. In subsequent chapters I will be discussing Erikson's views on moral development and ritual process.

A STAGE-BASED THEORY

From time to time Erikson has altered the names of some of his eight stages. The formulation in the chart given here is his most recent version, and it is very close to his original version (see figure A). The major substantive changes have occurred in the sixth and seventh stages. At times, Erikson has used the term "self-absorption" in place of "isolation" (young adulthood) and "stagnation" (adult-

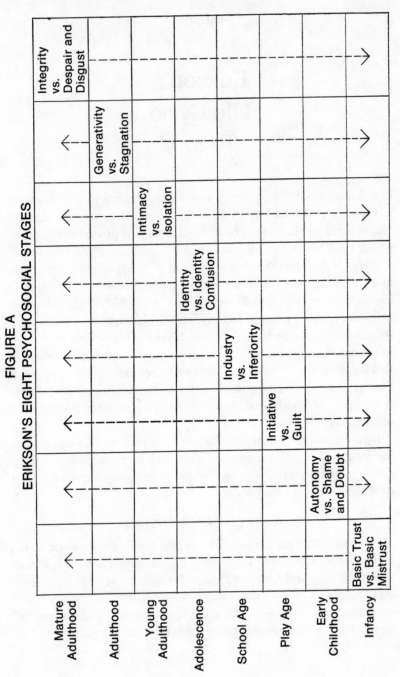

FIGURE A
ERIKSON'S EIGHT PSYCHOSOCIAL STAGES

hood). His latest version restores the original rendering of these stages as they were given in *Childhood and Society*.

The key concept in Erikson's theory is the idea that human development proceeds by stages. His life cycle charts depict development as a series of eight steps which a person "ascends" in chronological order. Unless there is premature death, we go through all the stages on schedule. The question is not *whether* but *how* one progresses through the appointed stages. Good progress at one stage increases our chances for good progress at the next stage, for positive growth is cumulative. But the reverse is also true: if one stage is poorly negotiated, we are more vulnerable to poor progress in the next stage. Some acceleration in progress from stage to stage is possible. Taking the first two stages as an example, the figure given here shows two alternative ways that an individual may progress from one stage to another (see figure B). We may linger excessively over basic trust and therefore move to autonomy (from I–1 to II–2) by way of I–2; or in an accelerated progression from basic trust we may move to autonomy (from I–1 to II–2) by way of II–1. This pattern of progress—and diversity—applies to the movement from any given stage to another.

FIGURE B

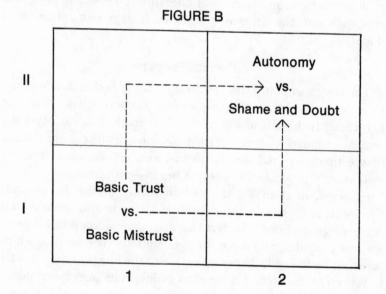

Erikson emphasizes that stages are left behind chronologically as we progress, but they are not left behind psychologically. For many people a particular stage exerts an uncommonly strong influence throughout their lives. Those who experience far too little or far too much trust in the first stage may be unusually preoccupied with trust issues throughout their lives, with the result that all subsequent stage crises raise new concerns about whom or what one can trust. In the same vein Erikson suggests that we may reexperience earlier stages. The adolescent, for example, may cycle back to the earlier stages to find new grounds for trust, autonomy, initiative, and industry. In his early writings Erikson used Ernst Kris's phrase "regression in the service of the ego" to describe this reversal.

These accelerations and regressions are possible because the stages are interdependent. The empty boxes in the eight-stages chart illustrate this interdependence. They show that each stage survives in the later stages (signified by the upward arrows), and the later stages reach down into the earlier ones (the downward arrows). Thus autonomy has its ascendency in stage 2, but there is already an element of autonomy in stage 1 (as illustrated by the infant's capacity to grasp someone's hand or push it away) and, like every other positive strength, autonomy continues through life. The same process applies to the negative pole of each stage (e.g., shame and doubt).

A Cyclical Process

The key concept in Erikson's theory is the idea that development proceeds by stages. Another important concept is that development is cyclical. In his discussion of the final stage, Erikson notes the semantic similarities between trust and integrity (the positive poles of the first and final stages).[4] Thus, in a certain sense, the developmental process ends where it began—with trust.

However, in clarifying the cyclical nature of the life process, Erikson focuses less on the individual life cycle and more on the "cycle of generations," the fact that each generation is interlocked with the preceding and succeeding generations. An educational film based on his life cycle theory makes use of the image of the carousel to represent the cyclical dimension of life in its intergenerational aspects. As the carousel makes its rounds, each individual goes through the eight stages of life, but a generational cycle is also taking place as new generations embark, old ones disembark, and the generations on board change their relationship to one another. Another image that Erikson uses to capture this cycle of generations is the cogwheel. This image depicts the interlocking of the generations as each follows its own cyclical pattern. It suggests that there are times when two generations are more closely linked to one another (as when children are growing up and in constant interaction with their parents) and other times when they are quite separate (as when children are grown and living apart from their parents).

In effect, Erikson uses both linear images (ascending staircase) and cyclical images (the circle of the individual life and the cogwheeling of the generations) to depict the life process. One way to reconcile these seemingly incompatible sets of images is to think of the life process as a wheel that goes around and around as it moves forward and upward.

Another circle which is crucially important to Erikson's life cycle theory concerns the social context in which the individual life cycle is embedded. Here Erikson uses the image of ever-widening concentric circles, like the circles produced by throwing a stone into a lake. In the first stage of the life cycle the infant interacts with the maternal person. With each successive stage the circle of social interaction widens. The second stage involves interaction with both parents; the third stage involves the whole family; the fourth stage adds the school and neighborhood; the fifth stage adds peer groups and outgroups; the sixth stage contributes partnerships; the seventh stage adds parenthood and enduring professional relationships; and the eighth stage contributes the most universal circle of all—identification with all humanity. Erikson concludes: "Personality can be said to develop according to steps predetermined in the human organism's readiness to be driven toward, to be aware of, and to interact with, a widening social radius."[5]

Bipolar Stages

An important conceptual feature of Erikson's life cycle theory is the fact that the stages are bipolar—*this* vs. *that*—with one positive and one negative pole. Erikson calls the positive poles strengths and the negative poles weaknesses. In his earlier writings he used the term "ego strength" to describe the positive pole of each stage, but in his later writings he has tended to downplay the term "ego" (with its specific psychoanalytic meanings) in favor of more general terms like "vital strengths" or "inherent strengths."

His use of evaluative terms like "strengths" and "weaknesses" has led to some misunderstanding. Despite his frequent cautionary warnings many people have thought that healthy growth simply involves achieving the positive strength and doing one's best to eliminate the negative weakness. But what counts is the *ratio* between the positive and negative poles. For healthy growth one needs a preponderance of the positive over the negative, but total elimination of the negative pole, even if it were possible, is undesirable. An individual who was wholly trusting and had no mistrust at all would be poorly prepared to function in a world which has its dangers and hostile elements.

Musical terminology is useful for describing the interaction between the positive and negative poles. Robert Coles says that the interaction between the two poles is similar to "trying to weave melodies, some that work and make good music, some that don't and in fact are noise or worse." He concludes that this interaction could be called contrapuntal.[6] Erikson himself uses the term "syntonic" to refer to the positive pole and "dystonic" to describe the negative one.[7] Following up on this, Joan Erikson, his wife, has constructed a weaving in which the syntonic elements are depicted in bright colors and the dystonic elements are depicted in gray strands which are interwoven with the bright colors. She says that the gray threads represent the dystonic elements "over which the colors must maintain their dominance and brilliance, as well as their essential characteristics."[8] Psychological strength requires a preponderance of the positive over the negative pole, but the negative pole adds a certain depth and complexity to the whole thematic pattern.

Epigenetic Ground Plan

By using images and metaphors to convey his life cycle theory, Erikson invites the impression that the theory is more like a work of art than a scientific construct. In fact, given his artistic background, he is more comfortable "painting contexts and backgrounds" than formulating scientific "concepts."[9] Still he wants to base his life cycle theory on a scientific foundation. His basic scientific concept is the epigenetic principle. This principle states that "anything that grows has a ground plan, and that out of this ground plan the parts arise, each part having its time of special ascendency, until all parts have arisen to form a functioning whole."[10] What this view of the growth process means is that (1) each stage is systematically related to all the others; (2) all stages depend on their proper development in the proper sequence; and (3) each stage exists in some form before its decisive and critical time normally arrives. When this time arrives, the individual has a "decisive encounter" with that segment of the social world that is of focal importance at this stage and the result is a "developmental crisis." Such crises are the inevitable effect of the destabilization that occurs when growth is taking place and each crisis forces "a radical change in perspective."

What accounts for these radical changes in perspective? Erikson contends that new perspectives on the world are due in large measure to radical changes in the "posture" from which the growing child perceives the world. The first experiences in childhood are "significantly related to the postural changes and modalities that are so basic to an organism destined to be upright—from proneness to crawling; from sitting and standing to walking and running—with all their resulting changes in perspective."[11] These new perspectives, in turn, make possible new forms of actively engaging the world. Erikson calls these forms "psychosocial modalities."

In stage 1, the infant first learns to "get" and "give in return." In stage 2, the child learns to "hold on" and to "let go." In stage 3, the child learns to "go after" things and other persons. In stage 4, the child learns to "make things." In stage 5, the adolescent learns to "be somebody." In stage 6, the young adult learns to "be with others." In stage 7, the adult learns to "take care of others." In stage 8, the mature adult learns "to be, through having been." Each new psychosocial modality reflects a radically new perspective on the world. As the child in stage 2, for example, begins to "hold on" and "let go" of things, the world becomes a place that is filled with objects and persons who lend themselves to "holding on" and "letting go." Our perspectives shape our capacity to encounter the world in new ways, and it is the epigenetic ground plan that causes these capacities to appear at prescheduled intervals and in a predetermined sequence.

A major implication of the epigentic principle is that this whole developmental plan can be hampered or thwarted by an inhospitable environment. A harmful social environment may inhibit or arrest growth in any given stage. The developing individual needs a hospitable environment in the "social radius" which is stage-critical, augmented by supports provided by environmental contexts that were critical at earlier stages. Children entering school age, for example, have critical need of a positive school environment, but they also require the more routine support of the home environment as their social radius undergoes this quite dramatic expansion. While the capacity for positive growth is inherent in the individual as part of the epigenetic ground plan, this capacity can be impeded or even thwarted under certain environmental conditions.

THE INDIVIDUAL STAGES

Erikson has described each of the stages in rather full detail, and there are also various books currently available that offer excellent interpretive analyses of the various stages.[12] Since the major focus of this book is not the process of individual development but the uses of Erikson's theory for clarifying the work of the pastor, I will summarize these stages very briefly.

Basic Trust vs. Basic Mistrust (Infancy)

Basic trust is an attitude toward the world and ourselves gained from our experience in the first year of life. It is a "reasonable trustfulness" toward others and a simple sense of trust in ourselves. It means we have learned to rely on the mothering person and have learned to exercise some control over our hostile urges. It does not depend on the total absence of frustration but on the quality of the maternal relationship.

Basic mistrust develops when the infant experiences the world, through encounters with the mothering person, as unreliable and unpredictable. It is especially evident in infants' attempts to manipulate the maternal person, insisting on her constant presence for fear that she will not return when genuinely needed.

Autonomy vs. Shame and Doubt (Early Childhood)

One- to three-year-olds can express their own will and therefore do battle for their own autonomy. On the one hand they want to "do it myself." On the other hand they want others to know that "you can't make me do it." Erikson relates this battle for autonomy to the child's new capacity to control arm, hand, and sphincter muscles. With this capacity the child can "hold on" and "let go" at will—grasping, dropping, and throwing things, clinging to possessions one moment and discarding them the next. The child struggles with conflicting passions: cooperation and willfulness, docility and assertiveness, submissiveness and obstinacy.

Shame and doubt are the negative poles of this stage. We often overlook the childhood emotion of shame because it is so easily absorbed by guilt. Shame is the experience of being exposed to the disapproving gaze of others. When subjected to excessive shaming the child tends to develop great inner rage or angry defiance of those doing the shaming. Doubt is reflected in excessive self-control. Instead of learning to express our will in interaction with others we stage interactions with others in advance, ensuring that these encounters are subject to neither variation nor chance.

Initiative vs. Guilt (Play Age)

In the previous stage self-will generally inspired acts of defiance or protested independence. In this stage initiative is added to autonomy, and the result is a new quality of undertaking. The child plans and "attacks" a task for the sake of being active and "on the move." The child's ability to walk with agility means being able to "get into things" with relative ease. Much of the initiative at this stage is intrusive in character, whether intrusion into space by vigorous movement, into other bodies by physical attack, into other people's ears and minds by aggressive talking, or into the unknown by a consuming, if sometimes ill-considered, curiosity.

The negative side of this stage is guilt. It emerges at this stage because the child is unable to impose appropriate limits on this intrusiveness and thus becomes a "transgressor." Some of this excess initiative is exuberance and natural curiosity, but some is aggressive and hostile, reflecting the child's feelings of rivalry and competition against other persons, especially parents and other siblings.

Industry vs. Inferiority (School Age)

By the time children enter school they are capable of applying themselves to skills and tasks. Through formal schooling children are initiated into the systematic use of tools and development of skills. When industry is developing normally, children are dissatisfied if they cannot make things and make them well. It is not enough that they feel well entertained. They want to feel productive and to win recognition by producing things.

The negative side of this stage is inferiority. It occurs when children's abilities or tools are unequal to the task they are performing, when they fail to achieve a desired social status among their peers, or when nothing they have already learned to do well seems to count for much with their teachers. It is also reflected in inhibitions due to an inadequate solution of conflicts from previous life stages. We may still want our mother more than we want knowledge and skill, or we may be inhibited from developing our own skills because we feel in competition with parents or older brothers and sisters.

Identity vs. Identity Confusion (Adolescence)

In this stage the consolidations achieved in childhood are breaking up. The upheaval is due to a rapidity of physical growth equal to that of early childhood (stage 2), and to the entirely new addition of genital maturity. Faced with this physiological revolution within, youths are confused about who they are and where they fit in. In the previous stages physiological growth impelled the child toward the positive pole of the crisis. In this stage it impels the adolescent toward the negative pole. In previous stages the body was an ally in the acquisition of positive vital strengths. In this stage the body is more the enemy, a source of confusion. In effect, identity confusion is the normative experience in adolescence and identity is that elusive but much-desired strength that we hope to wrest from this confused situation. Adolescents temporarily help one another through such confusion by forming cliques and by stereotyping themselves, their ideals, and their enemies.

Identity is the consciousness of being a "coherent self." It means having a sense of "I." Before adolescence, children are only dimly aware that they possess various selves, and hardly question the assumption that we are not one "simple" self. In adolescence, they become conscious of these various selves and have the sense that they are a totally different self as they move from one social context to another. To have an identity, then, is to have a sense of being "one self," of feeling that our many selves somehow hold together. The formation of this coherent self is achieved by discarding those selves which have the potential for being incorporated into our sense of "I" but which, after much struggle and anguish, are repudiated. These rejected selves constitute our "negative identity," which is not a "bad" identity in the moral sense but an identity that we eventually negate, deciding that this is not who we are. While painful this repudiation is necessary for clarifying what one *is*.

But the experience of developing a sense of "I" is certainly not all pain and misery. To experience oneself as an "I" is to have a subjective sense of being alive, perhaps for the first time. Adolescents often look back on their childhood with some disdain for the person they used to be: "I was nothing," "I was nobody," "I hardly existed." Sometimes this sense of being alive has the immediacy and awe-inspiring quality of a numinous experience. In fact Erikson makes an important linkage between one's consciousness of being a coherent self and one's consciousness of God. He uses the term "self" to capture our perceptions of who we are and who we envision ourselves to be. The self is our subjective sense of being "the center of awareness in a universe of experience."[13] Other selves, beginning with our mothers in our infancy, help to shape and confirm this sense of being a center of awareness. But God is the ultimate source of this perception of ourselves as centers of awareness, for God is the eternal center of awareness: "That is why God, when Moses asked Him who should he say had called him, answered: 'I AM THAT I AM.'"[14]

Intimacy vs. Isolation (Young Adulthood)

Real interpersonal intimacy is hardly possible until we have achieved a "reasonable sense of identity." This is because intimacy involves risking our newly achieved sense of identity, taking chances with what was most "vulnerably precious" in the previous stage.

Thus if the identity stage involved the formation of our self, the intimacy stage involves letting this self go in order to form shared identities with others.

The negative pole of this stage is isolation, which may be due to a reluctance to abandon ourselves out of a fear of self-loss, or to a need to repudiate other persons and groups because their identities seem dangerous to our own. A common form of isolation is the dyadic withdrawal, where a newly married couple withdraw into their own world and sever ties with the world around them. This withdrawal works against intimacy because it extends the self-protectiveness of the identity stage into the marriage relationship.

Generativity vs. Stagnation (Adulthood)

Generativity is concern for establishing and guiding the next generation. Raising our own children is the paradigmatic form of generativity, but generativity is not limited to child-rearing. The generative adult is anyone who is a constructive participant in the "cogwheeling" of generations, who is able to see beyond the preoccupations and interests of our own generation, and to focus on the needs of future generations. Real generativity reflects an altruistic concern for the care and nurture of others, but it also involves the mature adult's need to be needed: "The fashionable insistence on dramatizing the dependence of children on adults often blinds us to the dependence of the older generation on the younger one."[15]

In most of his writings Erikson uses the term "stagnation" to represent the negative pole of this stage. By stagnation Erikson means the loss of desire or inner motivation to perform acts of care and nurture, resulting in a perfunctory discharge of these responsibilities or the neglect of them altogether. In other writings Erikson uses the term "self-absorption," which is the basic cause of an adult's "sense of stagnation and interpersonal impoverishment." When self-absorbed, adults treat themselves as though they were their own children and thus devote much of their emotional resources to nurturing themselves rather than the younger generation. In his most recent writings Erikson has emphasized the relationship between generativity and control, as if to suggest that the most important issue now confronting generative adults is not the problem of stagnation (too little generativity) but control (the dangers of too much generativity). The two major forms of control being discussed today—birth control and arms control—are making possible new forms of generativity. The issue is no longer how to be generative but how to be generative within appropriate limits and in ways that are morally responsible to future generations.

Integrity vs. Despair and Disgust
(Mature Adulthood)

Integrity has two major attributes. The first is an acceptance of our life—which includes acceptance of the people who have been especially significant in our lives—and of the fact that our life is our own responsibility. If the identity stage involves discovering our sense of "I," the integrity stage means endorsing it. In his earliest accounts of the life cycle Erikson also emphasized acceptance of our death. In his more recent accounts acceptance of death is still emphasized, but now he distinguishes between a nonacceptance of the finality of death borne of despair and the desire to transcend the limitations of our own life cycle borne of "ultimate concern" (a term which he borrows from Paul Tillich). We need to accept the fact that death marks the end of our psychosocial identity, but the end of the cycle also evokes ultimate concern for what chance we may have to transcend the limitations of our identity.[16] For many persons, this transcendence means meeting the "Ultimate Other" face to face. Erikson quotes St. Paul in this connection: "Now we see in a mirror dimly, but then face to face" (1 Cor. 13:12). Such an encounter would, in some sense, recapitulate our encounter with the face of our mother (the "Primal Other") in the very earliest moments of postpartum existence.

The second attribute of integrity concerns our participation in the succession of generations. The previous stage involved care of future generations. This stage centers on one's comradeship with members of preceding generations, with various "men and women of distant times and of different pursuits who have created orders and objects and sayings conveying human dignity and love."[17] This reaching out to men and women of distant times is a reflection of the self's "proclivity for order and meaning—an emotional integration faithful to the image-bearers of the past."[18]

The negative pole of this stage is despair, which is often hidden behind a show of disgust, misanthropy, and contempt for other persons and institutions. There is also a self-contempt owing to little sense of comradeship with those whose lives and achievements mirror human dignity and love. This is a form of real disgust directed at oneself. Erikson worries that with the gift of increased longevity we will see vastly increased numbers of the despairing old. In times past the number of older persons in a society was much smaller, and they were accorded honor and respect for having achieved longevity. When old age is no longer considered an achievement for which an individual deserves special recognition and status, we are likely to see much more despair among the older generation.

THE ORIENTATION MOTIF

All developmental theories are concerned with change for it is axiomatic that as persons develop they change. What makes Erikson's life cycle theory distinctive is its strong emphasis on the importance of orientation in the process of change. Erikson asks: How does the individual acquire and maintain a sense of orientation in this ongoing process of change? Orientation language abounds in Erikson's writings. He talks about continuity, succession, order, rootedness, perspective, stability, balance. He takes none of this for granted. He has no illusions about life in modern society. He knows it is often discontinuous, disruptive, disordered, uprooted, and fragmented. But he stresses the importance of having a clear sense of orientation in life, a steady image of where we have been and where we are going. He rejects the romantic notion that disorientation and disorder are more "natural" to the human species and therefore more desirable or worthwhile.

Becoming oriented in the world is the basic issue in the three most critical developmental stages in Erikson's life cycle theory: infancy, adolescence, and mature adulthood. In these three stages the question of our orientation in the world is most pressing and insistent. In the first stage of life our basic orientation in the world is being formed; our mother's task is to help us begin to feel "at home" in the world. In the fifth stage of life adolescents are confronted with developing a sense of self, which means discovering a way of being in the world which is uniquely their own. In adolescence we begin to assume responsibility for "fitting into" our world. In the eighth stage we are confronted with the necessity of relinquishing our place in the world. We face the prospect of the "completion of life" in the world. These themes of being "at home," "fitting in," and "completing life" in the world are three fundamental ways of being oriented in our world, of knowing our place.

This orientation motif is the thread that runs through the following presentation. In the next chapter I will consider the disorienting effects of immorality (the deadly vices). This is the first of three chapters concerned with the three major causes of disorientation in our world: the loss of moral order; the sense that our lives fail to hold together in a meaningful, comprehensible way; and the experience of severe suffering.[19] Erikson's life cycle theory enables us to explore all three issues, and thus develop an understanding of pastoral care as response to the threat of disorientation in the world.

CHAPTER 2

The Moral Counselor

Erik Erikson made two major additions to his life cycle theory in the early 1960s. One was his "schedule of virtues,"[1] the other was his "stages in the ritualization of experience."[2] I will focus in this chapter on the schedule of virtues and its implications for the pastoral role of the moral counselor. Given my concern with the causes of disorientation in life, I will address Erikson's schedule of virtues from the perspective of the widespread absence of virtue in modern life. Thus the central focus here is my proposal of a schedule of vices to correspond to Erikson's schedule of virtues.

In our current enthusiasm for stage theories of moral development, we need to give more attention to the causes of arrested moral development. This means taking vices more seriously as impediments to the formation of moral character. Certainly Erikson's own schedule of virtues needs to be seen in dynamic interplay with corresponding vices, not as an effortless process of unimpeded moral growth. And certainly the disorienting effects of immorality need to be recognized and understood by pastors who seek to give sound moral counsel. Since vices cause such disorientation, they are not trivial or inconsequential.

SCHEDULE OF VIRTUES

Erikson develops the moral dimensions of his life cycle theory in his essay, "Human Strength and the Cycle of Generations."[3] Here he proposes a schedule of virtues to correspond to the eight stages of the life cycle. These virtues and their corresponding stages are hope (basic trust vs. basic mistrust), will (autonomy vs. shame and doubt), purpose (initiative vs. guilt), competence (industry vs. inferiority), fidelity (identity vs. identity confusion), love (intimacy vs. isolation), care (generativity vs. stagnation), and wisdom (integrity vs. despair and disgust). Some of these virtues, like hope, fidelity, love, care, and wisdom, are already in the Christian's lexicon of virtue. The others (will, purpose, and competence) are not as common but they have parallels in such Christian virtues as courage (will), dedication (purpose), and discipline (competence).

Erikson thinks of these virtues not as static traits but as inherent strengths that are cultivated in encounter. They become alive and vital through our interaction with persons and social institutions, especially those most decisively involved in our lives at that developmental stage. The maternal person is decisive for evoking the virtue of hope; parents are decisive for will; the family for purpose; the school for competence; peer groups for fidelity; marriage partners and friends for love; children, youth, and younger adults for care; and living traditions for wisdom. A virtue's effects, of course, are not limited to the chronological stage to which it corresponds. This is simply the stage in life when the particular virtue has its best chance to develop. The virtues also build on one another. In the virtues of childhood there is no will without hope, no purpose without will, no competence without purpose. In the virtues of adulthood there is no love without fidelity, no care without love, no wisdom without care. Thus Erikson warns that it is not enough to value these virtues individually. We also need to recognize that the virtues are linked to developmental stages. If this is not understood, our efforts to inspire virtue in our children and cultivate virtue in ourselves will be haphazard and arbitrary. Removed from its developmental moorings, Erikson's schedule of virtues becomes a mere list of virtues, and efforts to inspire and cultivate virtue become random and idiosyncratic, not truly formative.

SCHEDULE OF VICES

If Erikson is right about the major virtues, what about the vices? Are there vices that correspond to the developmental stages? I believe that there are. Like virtues, vices also follow a developmental sequence. At each stage in life a new vice appears and it, together with previous vices, hinders our efforts to give moral order to our lives. Erikson says that, whatever we might call the negative counterpart to virtue, its symptoms would have to be "disorder, dysfunction, disintegration, anomie." He doesn't like to use terms like "vice," "sin," or "character flaw" to describe this negative counterpart to virtue because they are too moralistic. But neither does he like the word "weakness" because it fails to account for the "complexity of disturbance" that occurs whenever we "are hindered in the activation and perfection of the virtues outlined here."[4] Recently, he has suggested that at each stage there is a basic antipathy which conflicts directly with the virtue of that stage. From the infancy stage through mature adulthood these antipathies are withdrawal, compulsion, inhibition, inertia, repudiation, exclusivity, rejectivity, and disdain.[5] While Erikson prefers to talk about antipathies, not vices, I believe that these antipathies foster vices. I will be focusing on the most serious of these vices. Incidentally, I use the term "vice" rather than "sin" because vices have traditionally been viewed as serious and persisting hindrances to virtue, while sins are thought of as individual acts of wrongdoing. However, the word "sin" is acceptable to me if it is meant to imply established attitudes and motivational patterns and not simply isolated acts of wrongdoing. My source for such vices (or sins) is the classical list commonly called "the seven deadly sins."

The Seven Deadly Sins

Ten years ago Seward Hiltner tried to resurrect this traditional classification, with its deadly sins of pride, greed, lust, anger, envy, gluttony, and sloth.[6] He suggested that Christians have abandoned this classification because it seems to place too much emphasis on external acts and not enough on our inner motivations, the "sinful attitudes" that give rise to sin. But he disputes this view of the traditional classification. The surprising fact, he says, is that "nothing in this list confines itself to isolated acts. Everything is characterological, related to tendencies of repetition. Acts are not absent, but they are implied to be inevitable consequences of tendencies of character."[7] Thus we need to take the "deadly sins" seriously, not because they involve occasional acts of wrongdoing but because they have major influence on the formation of moral character. In suggesting that we resurrect the traditional classification of sins Hiltner is not being moralistic or trying to restore a moral legalism in which specific acts are proscribed. He does not want a "return to a legalistic lockstep system of assessing penalties in this or that degree."[8] But he does say that we cannot tolerate the "illusion that, since all sin is sinful, let us therefore have no typologies at all."[9] In his judgment we need to distinguish types of sin and then study the long-term effects of these various sinful attitudes.

In a more recent study Brian W. Grant has again drawn attention to the seven deadly sins.[10] He too is concerned with the attitudes that underlie sinful behavior and takes the view that behind each sin there is a "good aim" that got distorted. Thus he advocates probing the attitudes behind sinful behavior so that we can discover what this positive aim is and develop more constructive ways to realize it. Grant also suggests that "we are always vulnerable to sins and sinning—but we can identify the points of greatest vulnerability to specific sins."[11] He proposes that the seven deadly sins are related to three developmental periods: the sins of a "falsely extended childhood" are sloth and gluttony; the sins of "misplaced adolescence" are anger and lust; and the sins of "exaggerated adulthood" are greed, envy, and pride. These sins are not limited to the period in which they emerge, for adults are certainly capable of all seven sins and the adult sins are found among children and adolescents. But when the sins of childhood and adolescence are found among adults they usually reflect the adult's resistance to adult maturity.

I will not take time here to discuss Grant's rationale for placing sloth and gluttony in childhood, anger and lust in adolescence, and greed, envy, and pride in adulthood. Instead I will propose my own model, based on a closer linkage of this traditional classification of sins (or, as I prefer to call them, vices) and Erikson's life cycle stages. If such a link can be demonstrated we will have achieved two major steps toward an understanding of how the vices inhibit moral formation. The first is that we can identify the psychosocial dynamics that produce a particular moral disorder. The second is that by noting the corresponding vices and virtues of each developmental stage, we can identify the virtue that is most likely to counteract a given vice.

Eight Deadly Vices

What about the fact that there are eight stages and only seven vices? I was struggling with this problem when I visited Professor

Erikson in December 1981, and I raised the question with him. He ventured the opinion that possibly there is no vice as such in the first stage of life, for moral conflict begins only with the second stage.[12] However, Joan Erikson, his wife, felt that gluttony had to be placed in the first stage of life; it was agreed that the problem could not be solved quite so easily. The solution was provided me by Stanford M. Lyman's book, *The Seven Deadly Sins*.[13] Lyman holds to the traditional seven, but he notes that sloth was originally two separate sins: indifference ("acedia") and melancholy ("tristitia"). These two sins were later merged by Gregory the Great who used the term "tristitia" to cover both. A later theologian, Alcuin, accepted this synthesis in principle, but in practice he used acedia rather than tristitia when referring to the sin of sloth because he felt there was positive merit in Christian sadness. By the later Middle Ages this sin was commonly understood as acedia, now called sloth, and tristitia, or melancholy, fell into disuse. I believe there is value in the distinction between indifference and melancholy and thus suggest that we think in terms of eight rather than seven deadly vices. Instead of sloth I use indifference and melancholy.

The schedule of vices that I propose is indicated in the accompanying table (see figure C). Reading down, the table suggests that gluttony, anger, greed, and envy are the vices that develop in childhood; pride emerges in adolescence; and lust, indifference, and melancholy arise in adulthood. Reading across, the table suggests that there is a direct link between the vice and virtue of a given stage, and between the vice and the psychosocial conflict and modality of each stage.[14] In discussing these linkages I will consider each vice in its behavioral form, then probe the attitudes behind the behavior. I will also indicate how the vice and virtue for each stage relate to one another, emphasizing that the virtue is the basic strength that breaks the grip of the vice in question.

THE INDIVIDUAL VICES
Gluttony (Infancy)

What is gluttony? Behaviorally, gluttony is an excessive, seemingly insatiable desire and capacity for engorging ourselves. Excessive eating and drinking are the most notable examples of gluttony. But gluttony takes many other forms as well. Some people have an

FIGURE C
SCHEDULE OF VICES

Psychosocial Conflicts	Vices	Virtues	Psychosocial Modalities
Basic Trust vs. Basic Mistrust	Gluttony	Hope	"getting"
Autonomy vs. Shame and Doubt	Anger	Will	"holding on, letting go"
Initiative vs. Guilt	Greed	Purpose	"on the make"
Industry vs. Inferiority	Envy	Competence	"making things"
Identity vs. Confusion	Pride	Fidelity	"being oneself"
Intimacy vs. Isolation	Lust	Love	"losing oneself"
Generativity vs. Stagnation	Indifference	Care	"taking care of"
Integrity vs. Despair	Melancholy	Wisdom	"to be, through having been"

insatiable desire for work; we say they are "workaholics." Others have an excessive capacity for taking abuse from other people; we say they are "gluttons for punishment." There are many forms of gluttony but, behaviorally speaking, what characterizes them all is an excessive desire and capacity to "take things in."

Why do people engage in gluttonous behavior? What attitudes lie behind such behavior? One important attitude that has direct bearing on infancy (especially the feeding process) is fear of future deprivation. This fear reflects mistrust. Infants feel that they cannot rely on the person who is responsible for their well-being to meet needs as they arise. To forestall this uncertain future infants try to get more than enough now, and in the process become demanding and manipulative.

Another important attitude behind gluttonous behavior is the discovery that the world is filled with objects that make us happy and contented. Infants discover that they are happy when they are well-fed and that they are unhappy when they are hungry. They associate happiness with the substance they are taking in. To discover that happiness occurs when something in the outside world enters the inner world is a remarkable insight (not unlike a numinous experience). But not all substances in the outside world have "good" effects when they are taken in. As infants and children gain more experience with "taking things in," they learn to discriminate between "good" and "bad" substances. Thus gluttony involves indiscriminate trust. It means taking in harmful substances that do not merit our trust. When we say that people are gluttons, we usually mean that they not only eat to excess but are also indiscriminate about what they take in. They are insufficiently suspicious of these substances, too willing to trust that these things will not cause irreparable harm. This explains why gluttony and addiction are closely related. An indiscriminate trust is the attitudinal link between them.

If gluttonous behavior reflects attitudes of mistrust and/or indiscriminate trust, what is the basic strength capable of breaking gluttony's deadly grip? The answer is hope, which Erikson defines as "the enduring belief in the attainability of fervent wishes."[15] If we have real hope we do not fear for the future, and therefore we do not need to secure an overabundance of supplies in the here and now. The hopeful individual trusts the future and is therefore able to "take the world in" with less desperation and greater discrimination. The hopeful individual is able to exercise a healthy mistrust. When we are hopeless and do not know or even care what the future holds, our ability to reject harmful substances is seriously impaired. Hope challenges the gluttonous illusion that "the world cannot hurt me because there is no tomorrow." Hope recognizes that there is a tomorrow, and that "how I receive the world today will have a powerful effect on how I will be oriented to the world tomorrow."

Anger (Early Childhood)

Behaviorally, anger takes many forms: physical abuse (hitting, wounding, killing), verbal abuse (shouting, humiliating, trenchant sarcasm), and self-abuse ("kicking" oneself). The attitude such angry behaviors have in common is an aggressive defense of an injured self. Anger is a response to assaults on one's dignity, threats to one's self-esteem, or status loss. When the self suffers injury, aggressive defense is a natural and sometimes effective reaction. Anger— "letting go"—informs one's assailant that one will not accept further injury: "I've taken enough from you." But oftentimes we internalize this anger. Rather than letting go, we hold the anger in and "smolder" or "fume" in silence. Erikson notes that children in the second stage of life often harbor a "secret rage" against parents who have subjected them to too much shaming. Such rage can be "held onto" only so long and then erupts in defiance (from "I can't take it anymore" to "I hate you for this").

Through the centuries Christians have been ambivalent about calling anger a vice. They point, for example, to the fact that Jesus threw the money-changers out of the Temple in a display of towering anger. In more recent years much emphasis has been given to the positive therapeutic value of "getting one's anger out." Is anger a vice or not? The answer Christians have traditionally given to this question is that anger is a vice if it undermines the kind of self-control that Jesus exhibited even in the act of expelling the money-changers. The answer to such anger is found in the virtue "will," which Erikson defines as "the unbroken determination to exercise free choice as well as self-restraint."[16] This means being able to exercise judgment and self-control in responding to an injury to ourselves. Instead of lashing out against our assailant in an uncontrolled outburst we develop the capacity to express or withhold our anger in a self-controlled fashion. This is one part of learning the difference between will and willfulness. The reason that a willed response is more virtuous than an uncontrolled lashing out is that it communicates our intention not to be deprived of our essential dignity and self-respect. Unlike the uncontrolled outburst (which often evokes derision or pity), a willed response to self-injury is a defense which in its very form and expression begins to restore our injured self.

Greed (Play Age)

Behaviorally, gluttony is limited by the finite capacity of the body ("If I eat any more, I'll burst"). But behaviorally speaking, greed has no limit. Greed is related to attainment, the achievement of certain goals, some of which are certainly above reproach and worthy of pursuit. But attitudinally, greed is an inordinate pursuit of these goals without respect for others—their well-being, their property, their feelings. Greed also tends to reflect an attitude of inordinate haste, an inability to work toward goals with steady perseverance. I must have it and have it *now*.

In terms of the psychosocial conflict of stage 3 greed is initiative which knows no limits. In terms of stage 3 modalities it is to be "on the make" with no sense of having to stay within any boundaries. Erikson calls this the "intrusive" stage because the child is always getting into things. Normally, however, parents place limits on the child's intrusions: "Don't go there." Or "Don't pick that up; you'll break it." Or "We are talking—don't interrupt." The child needs to be intrusive. It is absolutely essential for the child's development at this stage to be able to intrude—through locomotion, aggressive talking, and a consuming curiosity. But children also need boundaries for their own protection and for the protection of the well-being and property of others. When children violate these boundaries they need to learn that they have "trespassed" or "transgressed" (two common religious words for guilt). Greed knows no such boundaries. It operates on the principle that one's desires are subject to no limits whatsoever.

The virtue of *purpose*, which Erikson defines as "the courage to envisage and pursue valued goals,"[17] breaks the grip of the deadly vice of greed. Purpose is also related to attainment and achievement of goals. But unlike greed, it operates within limits. It does not run roughshod over others, violating their property and well-being. On the contrary, it fosters a collaborative spirit in which persons work toward common objectives. When purpose is present, the greedy pursuit of an objective is replaced by a spirit of exploration. Greed says: "I must have it. Give it to me." Purpose says: "That interests me. What is it for? How does it work?" Adults who supervise young children's play know what a difference there is between play based on greed and play based on purpose. When purpose prevails, there is mutual respect for the property, feelings, and dignity of one another. And purpose is not consumed by inordinate haste. The purposeful individual lays plans for the future and does not insist on having everything now. What the purposeful understand, and the greedy do not, is that planning actually enhances desire. The purposeful pursuit of a goal does not mean merely deferral of gratification, but clarification and intensification of desire.

Envy (School Age)

Envy is the desire or longing for what others possess, whether material possessions or personal qualities and capacities. When children enter school comparison between "my skills" and those of others is inevitable. Few children escape the sense of being inferior to others, because few children excel in everything. Also, in the school situation, children encounter persons (teachers and other children) who treat them as inferior even when they are not. Behaviorally, envy may take many different forms. Some children avoid children of whom they are envious, others seek ways to "cut them down to size," while still others make concerted efforts to associate with the child of whom they are envious in order to participate, vicariously, in that other child's superiority over others. Attitudinally, envy often involves the strong feeling that life is unjust ("Why is Mary so smart and I'm so dumb?"); envy often harbors the desire for revenge ("I hope Mary flunks the quiz").

However justified envy may be in any given situation, Christians through the centuries have recognized that envy is basically destructive to the envious person. This is because envy creates a pervasive feeling of impotence. When individuals become consumed with envy, this generally immobilizes them. They find they are unable to work up to their own potential or attain levels of performance of which they are clearly capable. Thus the virtue that corresponds to this stage is the opposite of impotence, namely competence, which Erikson defines as "the free exercise of dexterity and intelligence in the completion of tasks."[18]

In developing competence one acquires skills and mental capacities that provide a genuine sense of good workmanship and the satisfaction that goes with the experience of work well done. Competence has its own intrinsic value which is not threatened simply because others can do more difficult work, or because others receive greater social (extrinsic) rewards for work that is equally or less competent. This does not mean, of course, that the virtue of competence takes the place of social justice. There is no inherent virtue in accepting an unjust situation if it can be rectified. In fact the vice of envy often immobilizes persons and groups from working toward greater justice for themselves and others. Envy plays into the hands of those who want to maintain a system that is unfair or unjust. On the other hand, the virtue of competence can mobilize people to work for social justice.

Pride (Adolescence)

Behaviorally, pride takes the form of conceit, arrogance, and an air of self-satisfaction. Traditionally, it has also been linked to vanity, especially in one's dress and one's claim to physical attractiveness. Throughout the history of Christianity, Christians have warned one another about the special dangers of religious pride. They have stressed the importance of maintaining a humble spirit concerning their spiritual gifts and acts of Christian service. Attitudinally, pride is an excessive self-regard; it is self-centeredness, an inordinate preoccupation with self.

I have placed the vice of pride in the adolescent stage because the primary psychosocial task of adolescence is to form a sense of "I." This means that the adolescent is necessarily concerned with self to the point of being self-conscious. But the effort to discover a sense of "I" within one's myriad selves is very different from pride, an inordinate self-regard. Erikson opposes what he calls an "inflated self" and says that when he uses the term "ego identity" he is not talking about the "vain sense of a self-made Self."[19] Rather, he means a self-coherence, the sense of being a whole person. Thus the self-consciousness of adolescents may go in one of two directions: toward inordinate self-regard ("pride") or toward a coherent sense of self ("identity").

If pride means having a vain sense of being self-made, the virtue that is necessary in order to break the deadly grip of pride is fidelity, which Erikson defines as "the ability to sustain loyalties freely pledged."[20] In pride one is loyal only to oneself. In contrast, fidelity means to be true to oneself by being true to others. In fidelity we learn what it means (and costs) to be faithful to another. Thus fidelity is the moral dimension of faith and pride is the vice that poses the greatest threat to faith.

Teenagers are especially sensitive to issues of pride, including conceit, arrogance, status claims, vanity in physical appearance, and claims to religious superiority. They sense that in struggling against this formidable vice they are wrestling with basic issues of faith. Without a sense of "I" there is no real faith because faith is an encounter between one centered self and another. This means that an adolescent who is concerned with developing a "personal faith" is necessarily giving much attention to self-discovery, and there is sometimes a rather fine line between working at becoming a "centered self" and merely being "self-centered" (or under the sway of pride). The virtue of fidelity is important just at this point because it counteracts pride by creating the moral conditions (faithfulness to other selves) for a reversal from self-centeredness to a self centered in God, the ultimate Other Self.

Lust (Young Adulthood)

Behaviorally, lust is uncontrolled passion. Throughout the history of Christianity sexual passion has typically been understood as the paradigmatic form of lust. Frequently it has served as a metaphor for various other types of lust, such as the lust for power and fame.

Christians have traditionally viewed lust as a serious vice because it tends to master the whole person. All of our actions, thoughts, and feelings come under the sway of one sovereign interest. Lust has also been viewed as profoundly asocial because it monopolizes our energies and leaves us incapable of devoting ourselves to occupational tasks and social responsibilities not directly related to the object of our passion. Attitudinally, lust tends to be antagonistic. When it takes sexual form, it is a thinly disguised assault on another person. While professing genuine regard, even love, it actually reflects an antagonistic attitude toward the sex partner. Lust is precisely not an act of true intimacy because there is no intention whatsoever of "losing oneself" in another.

Lust is the vice of young adulthood because it masquerades as intimacy but is actually severely isolating. This is true not only of sexual lust but also of lust for power and fame. Lust isolates because of its essentially asocial character and here it contrasts sharply with love, the virtue of this stage, which Erikson defines as "mutuality of devotion" joining selves together in a "shared identity."[21] Because lust isolates, it is the quintessential vice. Of all the vices, lust makes clear most vividly that vices erect barriers against genuine encounter. Conversely, love is the quintessential virtue because, of all the virtues, it stresses the mutuality in genuine encounters. Furthermore, it is the most sensitive to the personal transformation that genuine encounters effect. In love we become what we were not and cease to be what we were. We relinquish our separate identities and gain a new shared identity. One major reason why Christianity has considered love the greatest of human virtues is that (in marked contrast to lust) it stands for personal transformation through mutual relationships with others.

Indifference (Adulthood)

Behaviorally, indifference is manifested in boredom and the paralysis of will. When we are under the sway of this vice our day-to-day activities seem irrelevant to any future and dissociated from any past. We are also incapable of reacting to new situations with appropriate energy. Our mind, emotions, and spirit are overcome by a great passivity. Indifference has sometimes been considered the most dangerous of all vices because it creates a favorable climate for the other vices, especially those that require much effort to resist. Attitudinally, indifference is a state of "not caring."

Indifference is the vice of adulthood, which is evident from the fact that the corresponding virtue is care. Indifference says, "I really don't care. I should care, but I don't." Adults, especially those in mid-life, often complain of their inability to take much interest in life anymore. They feel they have experienced everything there is to experience in life and the second half of life is shaping up as "just more of the same." Injustices at work, atrocities on the battlefield, a stagnating marriage, and other people's direct assault on the values one holds dear evoke "no reaction." Younger persons' appeals to them to make changes in "how things are done around here" are met with "we already tried that" or "I like your suggestion myself, but my colleagues would never go along." This indifference is also evident in the spiritual barrenness of adult lives. Adults may be going through the motions of religious life, but there is a profound emptiness inside.

Erikson addressed this feeling of inner vacuity in his controversial essay, "Womanhood and the Inner Space," and its sequel, "Once More the Inner Space."[22] This is not the place to discuss the controversy that the original article spawned or Erikson's response to feminist critics in the sequel. What *is* pertinent to the issue of indifference in adulthood is his use of the metaphor "inner space" to address the adult's need for generativity. In the original article he noted that one form of perdition, perhaps best understood by women but also experienced by men, is the feeling that one is "empty" inside. Physical barrenness is a metaphor for spiritual barrenness. And, like the inability to bear a child, what the spiritually barren miss are the "signs of life" moving inside oneself. Erikson strikes a similar note in *Young Man Luther*, where he describes Luther's understanding of Christ as God moving within him and therefore as God moving him to action.[23] In spiritual terms indifference is the sense that there is nothing moving in the inner space, no sense that God is moving us. We are literally "unmoved."

The virtue that breaks the deadly grip of indifference is care, which Erikson defines as "the widening concern for what has been generated by love, necessity, or accident."[24] Directed toward the young, care involves inculcating the virtues of hope, will, purpose, competence, fidelity, and love in the younger persons for whom the adult bears responsibility. Thus care is the adult virtue that makes it possible for children to develop their own virtues. It involves being moved from within, caring because we are moved to care. Because care is like this, it is the best example of the fact that the virtues are inherent strengths—not imposed from without but "generated" from within.

Melancholy (Mature Adulthood)

Behaviorally, melancholy is a world-weariness, often precipitated by loneliness and rejection. It manifests itself in feelings we generally subsume under the heading of despair. These include sadness, depression, misanthropy, peevishness, self-contempt, and contempt for others. Attitudinally, melancholy results from a withdrawal of emotional investment in a lost object. As Freud suggested in his famous essay on mourning and melancholia, one withdraws one's emotional investment from the lost object and then turns against it in anger or resentment.

Erikson's life cycle theory suggests that in the eighth stage of life we begin to withdraw our emotional investment in the world. This does not mean that we necessarily become reclusive and disengaged from life, but it does mean a certain withdrawal from many of the cares of life to which adults in the previous stage devote much of their time and energy. The withdrawal side of melancholy is not a vice, nor is the inevitable sadness that accompanies it. But vice does arise when melancholy turns against the object from which it is withdrawing. It is this hostile act that makes melancholy a vice. The world (and persons and things within the world) that we previously invested with interest and desire are now treated with disgust. In this hostile form of melancholy we are defending against loss by asserting that the lost object was unworthy of our previous investment.

The virtue that is capable of breaking the deadly grip of such melancholy is wisdom, which Erikson defines as a "detached concern with life itself in the face of death itself."[25] Wisdom is not without desire, but it is able to view objects of former desire with a degree of detachment that may be described as "loving from afar." Thus wisdom relinquishes investments in the world without turning against the world. Wisdom knows the sadness of melancholy but not its defensive attack on the objects of our sadness.

Vice as Negative Capability

Of course, these sketches of the major vices could be developed in much greater detail. But I trust I have said enough to support the view that these vices emerge in developmental sequence—epigenetically, as it were. Like the virtues in Erikson's schema the vices have their times of ascendency in the life cycle; this is what permits us to locate them in specific life stages. But they are certainly not limited to these stages. The childhood vices survive in adulthood and, when they are exhibited by adults, these vices often take much more menacing forms. Similarly, the adult vices are sometimes found among children. In fact, when the adult vices of lust, indifference, or melancholy are found to an inordinate degree in a child, we typically judge the child to be emotionally disturbed. Thus we ought not to think of the vices as stage-limited. We should view them instead as negative capabilities that are part of the epigenetic ground plan and thus always available to cause disorder, dysfunction, disintegration, and anomie.

THE PASTOR AS MORAL COUNSELOR

What does the foregoing schedule of vices contribute to our understanding of the pastor as moral counselor? I see at least two important contributions. First, it can assist the pastor in diagnosing the moral problem of an individual parishioner. We often make a purely psychological assessment of a parishioner's problem or situation and fail to consider the possibility that it is, at bottom, a moral problem.

A good illustration of this failure is a counseling case in Newman Cryer and John Vayhinger's *Casebook in Pastoral Counseling*.[26] The counselee is a parishioner who had served in the Korean War and five years later began physically abusing his wife. He understood that this was a delayed stress reaction to his war experience and felt it must have some connection with the night he killed five enemy soldiers in cold blood—stabbing each one in the back as they passed the thickets where he was hiding. He went to his pastor for help, and we have the following exchange:

> JOHN: Didn't bother me much at first, even when I came back from the war. Didn't bother too much. But then I got to thinking about it. All the time God says, "Thou shalt not kill." But I did. I killed—five of them—a knife right through each one.
>
> PASTOR: This has caused you some amount of worry since you have come back?

Notice how the counselee is describing his problem in moral terms ("I *killed* five men") while the pastor responds in purely psychological terms ("You are *worried* about this"). This pastor, though schooled in "reflective listening," is unable to respond to deep moral anguish with interpretive skill. What is needed here is the capacity to engage in genuine moral counseling, to help this war veteran gain moral clarity about an experience that has driven him to the limits of his moral insight and is now driving him to further vicious behavior in the physical abuse of his wife. John represents a case of stage 2 moral confusion. Moral diagnosis: uncontrolled anger in defense of an injured self. John says, in effect: "The war made me a cold-blooded killer. I can't believe this is who I am. Yet the facts don't lie." The focus of moral counseling: now that John is expressing his anger against the war's brutal assault on his previously positive sense of self, he needs to develop a *willed* response to this self-injury in place of the uncontrolled lashing out reflected in his abuse of his wife. It is impossible to determine from this single interview all of what this response might be. But we do know that his need is to restore his injured self and recover his dignity and self-respect, not further undermine it as his abuse of his wife is doing. One obvious place to begin is to pledge that he will refrain from further attacks on her until he and his pastor have been able to devise a long-range strategy of moral rehabilitation.

John served in the Korean War. But one would hope that the publicity now being given to the delayed stress syndrome among Vietnam veterans is sensitizing pastors to the fact that many of the problems we encounter as pastors are not simply psychological problems. They are problems of moral disorientation.[27] They are the problems of persons who have reached the limits of their own moral insight, persons who are asking not merely "What do I want out of life?" but "What should I do?" and "What, in God's name, have I done?" They seek moral counsel, but pastors often fail to give it because *they* have been counseled not to "give advice." In my judgment it is time for pastors to begin advising their parishioners (if they are not already doing so), sharing their own moral insights with people who desperately need moral counsel and look to the clergy for help. A working knowledge of the major vices and their corresponding virtues, and of the psychodynamics behind them, can be an important resource for the pastor who wishes to provide informed moral counsel.

A second contribution this schedule of vices can make to our understanding of the pastor as moral counselor is that it sensitizes us to the fact that many parishioners are leading lives of moral desperation. They are struggling to live up to their moral ideals but falling back into the grip of these deadly vices. Many pastors have been ambivalent about their parishioners' desire to lead "good, upright lives" because this desire has seemed a perversion of the Christian gospel, with its emphasis on justification by faith. But many Christians are struggling against their dispositions toward gluttony, anger, greed, envy, pride, lust, indifference, melancholy, and various other vices and are distressed at the havoc one or another of these vices is making of their lives. They want help, but many pastors are ill-equipped, more by virtue of their theological convictions than their lack of counseling skill, to provide the moral counsel these persons desperately need.

Moreover, our society is not much help. At best it views the deadly vices as somewhat trivial, as matters of poor taste, bad judgment, or personal eccentricity rather than impaired morality. At worst it touts these vices as genuine virtues. Our public servants, celebrities, and the media (to which many of us have a gluttonous attraction) are constantly rationalizing vices as virtues. This goes for the vices of conspicuous consumption (gluttony, greed, and lust) and the vices of self-absorption (anger, envy, pride, indifference, and melancholy). Thus many people have been led by the social and cultural climate of our times to underestimate just how deadly these vices can be until they find themselves controlled by them. Then they discover that the vices are truly demoralizing.

Can pastors do more to help their parishioners with their moral concerns, especially those persons who will not come to their pastors for personal counseling? One area where pastors can do more is through their preaching. Certainly, many pastors already use the pulpit for providing moral counsel. But perhaps we can be more intentional about the role of moral counseling in preaching. In *A Psychology for Preaching* Edgar Jackson tells of an experiment carried out in a local congregation whereby the pastor alternated from Sunday to Sunday between two types of sermon for sixteen weeks.[28] The first type of sermon was inspirational, intended to provide external support to help parishioners face the unpleasant realities of life. The second was analytic, designed to help parishioners discover the inner resources that they themselves possessed to deal with life realistically and competently; these sermons encouraged self-examination. Both types of sermon have moral significance, but the second type was clearly a sermon of moral counsel. The study revealed that the first type evoked a sense of joy and communal spirit among the parishioners, while the second type created a mood of uncomfortable introspection and self-examination with little communal spirit and some antagonistic feeling toward the pastor. Yet the analytic sermon was much more likely to prompt individuals to want to talk to the pastor about the personal problem, with the largest single response coming after a sermon on envy.

This experiment suggests that there is real interest among parishioners in sermons that offer moral counsel, but that care—the virtue of the generative adult—must be exercised in implementing this approach. A steady diet of sermons that invite parishioners to look at their lives from a moral perspective would have a damaging effect on the morale of the congregation as a whole. But the overwhelming response of individual parishioners to the analytic sermons, especially the sermon on the deadly vice of envy, indicates that sermons of moral counsel have a vital place in the pastor's homiletical repertoire.

I conclude with an episode from the life of Benjamin Franklin. Writing in his autobiography, Franklin acknowledges that he did not attend church regularly, but did attend the Presbyterian church from time to time because the minister, a friend of his, asked him to do so. At one point he attended "five Sundays successively." But he found the sermons "dry, uninteresting, and unedifying, since not a single moral principle was inculcated or enforc'd, their aim seeming to be rather to make us Presbyterians than good citizens." The last straw for Franklin was a sermon based on Phil. 4:8: "Finally, brethren, whatsoever things are true, honest, just, pure, lovely, or of good report, if there be any virtue, or any praise, think on these things" (KJV, author paraphrase). Franklin says: "And I imagin'd, in a sermon on such a text, we could not miss of having some morality." But the sermon centered on these five points: keeping the Sabbath holy, diligence in reading the Scriptures, regular attendance at public worship, partaking of the sacrament, and paying due respect to God's ministers. Franklin complains: "These might be all good things; but, as they were not the kind of good things that I expected from that text, I despaired of ever meeting with them from any other, was disgusted, and attended his preaching no more." Franklin resumed his own private worship at home and began to devise his own "bold and arduous project of arriving at moral perfection," focusing on thirteen virtues.[29]

Our initial reaction may be that Franklin was merely rationalizing his desire to stay home from church on Sunday morning. But the more we think about it, the more sympathetic we may become. Franklin had the right to expect that at least one sermon in five would have "some morality" in it. I suspect that many Christians today are having to do what Franklin did—devise their own projects—to work toward a more virtuous life and combat the vices that bedevil them, without much explicit encouragement from their pastors.

On the other hand, pastors have not been encouraged to view themselves as moral counselors. The result is that even in their pastoral counseling they have not been "giving counsel." This is why I have taken pains in my model of pastoral care to differentiate the roles of moral counselor and personal comforter. In chapter 5, where I develop this model in systematic fashion, I will be viewing the Book of Proverbs as an important biblical foundation for this emphasis on the pastoral role of moral counselor.

CHAPTER 3

The Ritual
Coordinator

In the early 1960s Erik Erikson developed a stage theory of ritual corresponding to his eight stages of the life cycle.[1] He has since expanded on this original formulation in his *Toys and Reasons*[2] and *The Life Cycle Completed*.[3] This extension of the basic stage theory in the direction of ritualization opens a challenging vista for pastoral care. It sensitizes us to the role that ritual plays in the everyday life of the church and draws attention to the various elements of this ritual process. From a pastoral standpoint it invites us to consider the pastor's role as "ritual coordinator." This chapter focuses on Erikson's theory of ritual and what it means for the pastoral role of ritual coordinator.

RITUAL IN THE PARISH

The word "ritual" brings to mind formal religious observances, ceremonies, sacraments, and liturgies. But most social-scientific experts on ritual say that we cannot limit the term to these formal rites, that we must expand it to include the ritualization of the everyday life of a community. Erikson agrees. He identifies two forms of ritual: (1) special rituals and rites, and (2) the ritualized customs of everyday life. Special religious observances like Easter are examples of the first type, while the use of a prepared agenda in a committee meeting and the greeting of family members when they enter the house are examples of the second.

Parish life has both types of ritual. Churches have regular morning services and various special rites such as baptisms, weddings, and funerals. They also have their "everyday" ritualized customs. Every congregation is ritualized through after-church coffee hours, pastoral visits to the sick and homebound, annual stewardship drives, and many, many similar activities. In *Worship as Pastoral Care* William H. Willimon addresses the first type of ritual.[4] I will be addressing both, but emphasizing the second type. The implications of this second type for pastoral care are a little more difficult to identify, mainly because the ritualized customs of everyday church life are so many and so seemingly diffuse. But Erikson's "stages of ritualization" are useful for helping us better to understand and to do pastoral care through the ritualization of everyday church life.

What does the ritualization of everyday church life have to do with pastoral care? There is widespread agreement among pastors today that pastoral care is not limited to pastoral counseling or, for that matter, to the care of individuals. We agree that it has something to do with the care of the "church," here understood as the parish or congregation. Yet we have had considerable difficulty over the years in conceptualizing this aspect of pastoral care. We recognize its great importance yet find it hard to talk about in any intelligent fashion, mainly because we lack the necessary conceptual models. Over the years some useful models have been proposed, including field theories and systems theories.[5] But by and large these models have not caught on with the great masses of pastors working in the local church setting.

I have no way of knowing whether my proposed use of Erikson's ritualization theory will catch on either, but most pastors who have discussed it with me have found it a useful conceptual model. Most have felt that its value is not so much in telling them things they did not already know about running a parish, as in helping them put this knowledge into a conceptual framework.

I use the term "ritual coordinator" to describe the pastor's role in this conceptual model. The ritual coordinator is the one who assumes responsibility for integrating the various ritual processes in the total life of the parish community, assisting it in shaping its ritual elements into a coherent and meaningful whole. The goal of the ritual coordinator is not to make the church into a smooth-running organization but to form a community that has a clear sense of its basic orientation both within itself and in the world. This chapter is concerned with how the pastor goes about working toward this goal.

ERIKSON'S THEORY OF RITUALIZATION

Erik Erikson was trained in the Freudian tradition, but his approach to ritual is quite different from that of Freud. In his major essay on the subject of ritual Freud made a comparison between religious rituals and neurotic obsessions (such as compulsive hand-washings);[6] he argued that both are examples of the human compulsion to repeat unresolved conflicts, and he contended that if those who engage in them could achieve insight into these conflicts, they would no longer need to repeat the ritual. Erikson acknowledges that neurotic obsessions look like religious and other "true" rituals, but he contends that this is because they are a "parody" of such rituals. Neurotic rituals are carried out in "tortured solitude" while religious rituals are social. In religious ritual there is interaction between ritual actors and there are shared meanings. Since neither of these essential features of religious ritual is present in neurotic obsessions, Erikson contends that rituals cannot be usefully compared to neurotic obsessions.[7]

While Erikson discusses a number of religious rites in his studies of Native American cultures, he takes particular interest in the ritualization of everyday life, focusing on its role in the socialization of the individual. To him ritualization is a resource that societies use to integrate their young into their life style and world view. From birth on it proceeds virtually without interruption, its major purpose being to orient individuals to the world around them. In a statement that serves as a working definition Erikson says that ritualization is "a creative formalization which helps to avoid both impulsive excess and compulsive self-restriction, both social anomie and moralistic coercion."[8]

The key to Erikson's whole theory of ritual is the idea that ritualization assumes new forms as individuals progress through the life cycle. Each of the eight stages of the life cycle contributes its own distinctive type of "creative formalization." His model of ritualization includes the following: (1) the names of the eight elements of ritualization corresponding to the eight stages of the life cycle; (2) the form of social encounter through which each ritual element is actualized; (3) the actual or potential disorienting experience which each stage in the ritualization process addresses; and (4) the ritual excess to which each stage is susceptible and which causes either social anomie or moralistic coercion. (By noting ritual excess, Erikson addresses the pathology issue that was foremost in Freud's mind when he linked neurotic obsessions and religious rituals. However, Erikson's schedule of ritual excesses focuses not on neurotic distortions of rituals by individuals but on the perversion of each stage's contribution to the ritualization process by the community. When such perversion occurs what is meant to be a creative formalization of the community's life together is undermined. Erikson calls this a form of "social pathology.") The accompanying table schematizes this model (see figure D).

RITUALIZATION IN CHURCH LIFE

In the following discussion I will first summarize Erikson's commentary on each ritual element and then suggest ways that it is directly relevant to the ritualization of everyday church life. In making these links to church life I will emphasize the pastor's role as ritual coordinator in those features of church life that are most relevant to the ritual element in question.

The Numinous Element (Infancy)

This scene is repeated each day in households with newborn babies: As soon as she greets her infant, who has just awakened with a cry, the mother goes into action searching for possible sources of the baby's discomfort. Erikson says that this "daily event is highly ritualized."[9] Day after day the mother repeats "a performance arousing in the infant predictable responses, which, in turn, encourage her to proceed."[10] Erikson views this ritualized event as the "ontogenetic source" of the numinous experience, which is "the devotional element in all periodical . . . observances."[11] In explaining this link between the greeting ritual and the experience of the numinous he notes that the infant has a need both "to be gazed upon by the primal parent and to respond to the gaze" and "to look up to the parental countenance and to be responded to." Thus the infant looks "for somebody to look up to, somebody who will, in the very act of returning his glance, lift him up."[12] When this need is responded

FIGURE D
ERIKSON'S STAGES OF RITUALIZATION

Psychosocial Stages	Ritual Element	Form of Encounter	Disorienting Experience	Ritual Excess
Basic Trust vs. Basic Mistrust	Numinous	mutual recognition	separation and abandonment	Idolism
Autonomy vs. Shame and Doubt	Judicious	trial	approval/ disapproval	Legalism
Initiative vs. Guilt	Dramatic	drama and story	self-condemnation	Moralism-Impersonation
Industry vs. Inferiority	Formal (Technical)	methodical performance	incompetence	Formalism
Identity vs. Confusion	Ideological	solidarity of conviction	selflessness	Totalism
Intimacy vs. Isolation	Affiliative	mutuality in work, friendship, love	exclusion	Elitism
Generativity vs. Stagnation	Generational	care for others	irresponsibility	Authoritism
Integrity vs. Despair	Integral	personification of ritual wisdom	incoherence	Dogmatism-Sapientism

to, there is a "face-to-face" recognition, and the baby is called by name. Erikson says that this ritual of being lifted up and called by name is very much like the numinous experience in the religious life. In the numinous experience we are recognized by God, called by name, and lifted up to God's embrace or loving gaze. Dynamically, such numinous experiences overcome our sense of separation and abandonment, the disorienting experience of the first stage of ritualization.

Erikson says that religion is the primary locus of the numinous in society, though frequently the political realm (with its emphasis on the leader "smiling charismatically from the placards") competes with religion for jurisdiction over the numinous. He also points out that the concern of religion to ritualize the numinous may be carried to excess, in which case we have idolism—the insistence that God, like the mother, always be visible. Erikson sees this as a manipulative attempt to eliminate all sense of separation from and abandonment by God. Some separation and abandonment is unavoidable in the religious life. Religions recognize this when they insist that the presence of God is not coterminous with our images or representations of God. The goal of true ritualization in this stage is not the total elimination of the sense of separation and abandonment but regular and consistent assurance that our separateness has been transcended (through face-to-face recognition and being lifted up) and our distinctiveness confirmed (through being called by name).

How does the ritual element of the numinous relate to ritualization in the church? We can immediately see its role in the special rituals and rites of the church. In baptism one is lifted up to God and introduced to God by name. In holy communion we recognize God in the bread and wine and are assured that God in turn recognizes us. The numinous is also reflected in the funeral service, both in the fear and anxiety of death (the "mysterium tremendum") and in the spirit of the deceased being lifted up to God (the "mysterium fascinans"). Noting a medieval depiction of Mary's death, where God is shown holding Mary's spirit in his arms like a swaddled baby, Erikson observes: "This closes the cycle of the first stage as projected on the whole of existence."[13] In death the life cycle comes full circle, and this is reflected in the ritual of the funeral.

But what role does this ritual element play in the ritualization of the church's everyday life? Here I would suggest that it especially concerns the parishioners' need to be recognized by face and by name. This recognition may take a variety of forms. There are greetings in the narthex of the church before and after the morning service, and there are informal exchanges (such as exchanging the peace) during the service. Mutual recognition is also ritualized in informal social gatherings such as coffee hours after church, or conversation before and after committee meetings, study groups, and other smaller gatherings. In these encounters individuals "recognize" one another and help each other to feel wanted and at home.

The pastor's role as ritual coordinator is to see that such recognition occurs and that it means not only overcoming our separateness but also having our distinctiveness confirmed. The critical element in recognizing a member is discernment of this person's distinctiveness within the community. Members' need for confirmation of their distinctiveness is poignantly reflected in their complaints that "No one bothered to ask me how *I* wanted to serve the church," "People treat me as just an extension of my wife," and "To the adults around here, the youth are just a lot of faceless kids."

Each congregation has its own style of ritualizing the numinous. My purpose is not to suggest specific initiatives for addressing the needs reflected in this ritual element. But I will say that the pastor is clearly the focal person here, and members' need for confirmation of their distinctiveness must be addressed by the pastor directly, not only through delegation of responsibility to committees and lay leaders. Pastors are not parental figures, but there is a sense in which the pastor needs to function like the mother in the mother-infant relationship because pastors are mediators of the presence of God. It should also be noted that we are dealing here with deep and basic needs. Members desiring to be recognized and to have their distinctiveness affirmed are not indulging some crass narcissistic urge. Rather they are expecting the church to perform the basic function of religion in any society, that of orienting them to the numinous.

The Judicious Element (Early Childhood)

The ritual element that emerges in the second stage of the life cycle is the judicious. Erikson calls it this because it introduces the growing infant to a new experience—approval and disapproval.

The parental voice which the infant now hears is not only the voice of recognition and reassurance but also the voice of approval for good deeds and of disapproval for bad or shameful deeds. Disapproval is typically communicated through shaming as the infant, previously accustomed to looking for mother's face, is now being asked to "look at yourself." Dynamically, this ritual form centers on the trial. The infant is viewed as a "culprit" whose bad deeds have been found out and is now being "exposed" as a shameful example to others, such as younger and older siblings who might otherwise be tempted to enact the same deeds. In the judicial trial in which adults engage there is the same basic intention of shaming the accused by exposing their deeds to public scrutiny and isolating them from the other people about them. But trials in a society are not limited to the judicial setting. They occur in all kinds of social settings, such as the dating process prior to marriage, tests and examinations in school, and evaluations of job performance.

The ritual excess in this stage is legalism, the victory of the letter over the spirit. Erikson says that such legalism may be expressed in a "vain display of righteousness or empty contrition" by the accused or by the accuser's "moralistic insistence on exposing and isolating the culprit whether or not this will be good for him or anybody else."[14] In its more extreme forms legalism involves moralistic sadism (taking great pleasure in inflicting pain on the culprit) and voyeurism (taking pleasure in seeing the culprit exposed).

In the history of the church the judicious element of ritualization has been the central feature of certain rituals and rites including excommunication hearings, heresy trials, and public examination of aspirants to membership or special status (such as ordination examinations).[15] It still remains, usually in much-truncated form, in the reception rites for new members. But we are concerned here with the role this ritual element of the judicious plays in the everyday life of the church. Here it is found especially in the way members express their approval and disapproval of the pastor. Much of the approval and disapproval dynamic of a congregational community focuses on the pastor, as laity express what they "like" or "don't like" about the pastor's performance and personality. A major part of the pastor's role as ritual coordinator is to devise ways in which disapproval of the pastor can be "creatively formalized" so that the ethos of the church does not degenerate into a "moralistic insistence on exposing and isolating the culprit whether or not this will be good for him or anyone else."[16] Each congregation has its own methods for dealing with disapproval of the pastor, and my purpose is not to propose any specific method here. But we should note well the term Erikson uses to refer to this ritual element. Unlike the term "judicial," the term "judicious" implies the exercise of wisdom and discernment in the expression of disapproval. Otherwise there is the danger that evaluation of the pastor will become legalistic in tone and substance.[17]

The judicious element also plays an important role in the congregation's response to prospective members. These persons are often made to feel that they are on trial. Many churches have difficulty formalizing the transition from trial to membership. Since an important cause of membership loss is geographical mobility (that is, people failing to become members of any church in their new location), this matter of response to new people is an important issue for every congregation. My purpose again is not to suggest specific strategies for individual congregations. But the judicious element suggests that we should be especially attentive to the potentially damaging effects of a prolonged "trial" period and/or excessive "exposure" as a visitor, especially if these are attributable to neglect, procrastination, or insensitivity. Becoming a member should be less of a "trial" than it is in many congregations if this can be done without trivializing a solemn commitment, because this particular type of trial is usually not a productive or instructive form of exposure.

The Dramatic Element (Play Age)

The ritual element associated with stage 3 is the dramatic. In this stage, children learn how to see themselves in dramatic terms. Through play with toys and through the fantasy afforded by storytelling, children experiment with self-images and imagine themselves as "ideal actors in an ideal plot."[18] They begin to identify with heroic and otherwise superior personages and in this way experiment with their own future roles. Through imaginative play and stories the child is presented with examples of both "ideal" (heroic) and "evil" (villainous) roles. Since the child often finds an evil role strangely appealing, this ritual activity evokes the experience of self-condemnation and inner guilt. If the guilt becomes overwhelming the child may abruptly terminate the play because the major function of play is to reinforce positive, ideal self-images.

In *Toys and Reasons* Erikson views the ritual excess as impersonation. Here children believe that they actually possess the qualities of the ideal person or role and use this self-idealization to control or manipulate others. Among adults impersonation involves "role-playing in the stage of reality"[19] in ways that are dangerous, physically or psychologically, to self and others. In *The Life Cycle Completed* Erikson views the ritual excess as moralism, which he defines as a "moralistic and inhibitive suppression of playful initiative in the absence of creatively ritualized ways of channeling guilt."[20]

How does the dramatic ritual element relate to church life? One special rite related to this ritual element is confession. Confession may serve the important purpose of enabling individuals and groups to channel their guilt in a creatively ritualized way. But it can also foster impersonation, the pretense of being truly repentant, and moralism, viewing the moral life as a matter of merely inhibiting bad intentions rather than liberating good intentions.

We are concerned here, however, with ritualization in the everyday life of the church. Here the dramatic ritual element gets at what we commonly call active involvement. It means assuming a "role" in the drama of this congregation, signifying one's interest in "taking part" and "doing one's part." In more personal terms it means merging our own life story with the life stories of other members of the congregation and with the congregation's "master story" as it has evolved through the succession of generations that comprises its history. Like play to the child the church offers its active participants a "microreality" in which they can "relive, create, and re-create past experiences, and anticipate future roles and events with the spontaneity and repetitiveness which characterize all creative ritualization."[21] Involved members are able to use the various interest and service groups, as well as the special projects of the congregation, to create a new past for themselves and rehearse a different future from the one they would otherwise have projected for themselves. For instance, an adult who has experienced severe rejection in childhood and youth may find acceptance through participation in a group that visits patients in a nearby mental hospital. A member who does not know what to do about her aging mother is able to discuss her dilemma during a break at choir rehearsal. Through these and many other involvements in the ongoing drama of the congregation, individuals gain new perspectives and insights into their personal story—past, present, and future.

One ritual excess to which such personal involvement is subject is impersonation, where individual participants and even whole groups of participants engage in various destructive forms of pretending to be what they are not. ("Impersonation" is a more suggestive term for getting at this pretense than the more judgmental term "hypocrisy.") Consider for example the marriage encounter group that stated its purpose was to help strengthen the marriages of its members but allowed the group meetings to undermine these very marriages. This group was engaged in impersonation, pretending to be what it was not. As ritual coordinator the pastor needs to help the congregation regulate itself, to assess whether such instances of impersonation pose serious dangers to those who are engaged in it, to other members of the church, or to the wider community.

Personal involvement is also subject to moralism, where the interaction between individual participants is inhibited, lacking the liberating "power of human playfulness."[22] Such inhibition is reflected in service and interest groups that assume it is wrong to play with ideas or to carry out their tasks and purposes with a measure of playful freedom. Paul Pruyser says that religion may be a "serious craft," but it is certainly "not without playful features."[23] Peter Berger views play as a "signal" of divine transcendence because "in joyful play it appears as if one were stepping not only from one chronology into another, but from time into eternity."[24] This suggests that when a church committee or group allows itself a degree of playful abandon in defining and implementing its goals, it experiences in that very freedom the liberating presence of God.

The dramatic ritual element is also reflected in a member's voluntary but typically guilt-inducing withdrawal from certain involvements in the church. This withdrawal can have many different meanings (as can the child's decision to terminate play), and there is always the danger that we will misdiagnose the motives of those who have chosen to quit because *we* choose to view their action from a moralistic perspective. But the dramatic ritual element suggests two possible reasons for such withdrawal that we often overlook.

One motive for such withdrawal has to do with the impersonation issue. Some parishioners sense that to continue in what they have been doing in the church would be to play a role which is no longer an accurate reflection of their understanding of the Christian story. While it is customary to view such withdrawal as a loss of commitment or a case of burnout, the real story is almost invariably more complex. If pastors can step down from their position as offended director of the church's performance and assume the more modest (and liberating) role of ritual coordinator, they will be in a much better position to listen with genuine attention as parishioners explain why they can no longer deliver their lines.

A second motive for withdrawal is to plan for future roles. Some parishioners withdraw from one form of involvement because consciously or unconsciously they want to take on other roles recognized or envisioned by the Christian faith. Erikson's observation that Martin Luther "grew elatedly into his role of reformer"[25] suggests that sometimes persons who are disengaging from one role are searching for a new role. Because they may themselves advance a conventional or trivial motive for their withdrawal, we may fail to see that such persons want not less involvement, but a different form of involvement. Strategies for dealing with such withdrawal will depend on the special circumstances of these individuals. But the implications of this form of withdrawal for the pastor's role as ritual coordinator are clear. The pastor needs to help the congregation create a community ethos in which members are actively encouraged to envision new roles for themselves, especially roles that are more congruent with their sense of "I" within the Christian story.

The Formal Element (School Age)

The ritual element that corresponds to the fourth stage is the formal, best represented in the methodical performance. This ritual element is fostered most of all by schooling. Schooling involves the ritualization of method and technique as greater attention is paid to the formal and technical aspects of what we are doing. Without this new element of ritualization the elements of the first three stages "would lack a binding discipline holding them to a minute sequence of competence acts and an overall quality of craftsmanship and perfection."[26] The disorienting experience which this ritual element addresses is a sense of incompetence, the feeling that one is unable to live up to the demands of "the physical performance and mental discipline required for the basic techniques taught."[27] This ritual element is subject to excess when it becomes formalistic, where methods and techniques are overly formalized, too perfectionistic, and given to empty ceremonialism. When this happens there is the danger that we will equate technique with truth and sacrifice all other values to proficiency. Throughout his writings Erikson warns against the dangers of excessive faith in technology.

This ritual element is reflected in the formal church-school program which enjoys the status of a "rite" in most congregations. But we are concerned with the ritualization of everyday church life. Here I would draw attention to the importance of discipline in the total ethos of the church. What the congregation needs to reflect in every aspect of its life is the discipline that we associate with the educational process. This does not mean that the church must be formal in the sense of being austere and unfeeling. It simply means that the church's communal life needs to reflect serious attention to matters of method and technique. This applies to every facet of the church's work together from the singing of hymns through the delivery of and response to sermons to the church's evangelistic outreach and moral reflection.

The ritual excess here is formalism, an excessive reliance on proficiency for proficiency's sake. Erikson describes this as "craft-idiocy,"[28] where for the sake of proficiency a person will neglect the human context within which this proficiency functions. This is a danger to which the minister and other skilled professionals employed by the church are especially prone. Good performance that is insensitive to the context in which it occurs is not good work. As Erikson says of Luther, "His style indicates his conviction that a thing said less elegantly and meant more truly is better work, and better craftsmanship in communication."[29]

This draws our attention to a symptom of formalism to which church life is particularly susceptible, namely ceremonialism. While we can identify it quickly when we see it in the worship service, it is often difficult to detect in the everyday ritualization of the church. One of its more subtle forms involves the "ceremony" we employ to ensure that we will not become formalistic, such as the almost compulsive informality of much congregational activity. Churches are prone to what Richard Fenn calls "uneventful speech." The ceremonialism that he finds in the seminar format in university life has also found its way into the churches. Consider his description of the seminar and see if it does not also fit the life of the church:

> There is virtually no single, direct statement of a personal vision that compels response. Relatively few of the speech-acts express strong feelings. . . . The expression of wishes is muted, and feelings or ideas are rather blandly reported. Indeed relatively few speakers respond directly to what others have said.[30]

Fenn says that what is missing here is the language of "real desire." Speakers talk, but they do not communicate what they really desire or long for, what they truly want to happen. A symptom of our inability to express real desire is reflected in our rather desultory, ceremonial use of petitionary prayer.[31] What Fenn draws attention to is the need for discipline in our communication with one another. Discipline means developing a style of speaking and acting that is "meant more truly." Responsiveness to the human context means avoiding overformalism. But it also means breaking out of the ceremonialized vacuity that renders the church's life "uneventful," and its communication "meaningless."

The Ideological Element (Adolescence)

The fifth stage of the life cycle adds two distinct types of ritual. There are the "spontaneous rites" by which adolescents ritualize their relationships to peers and differentiate themselves from adults and younger children. And there are the "formal rituals of graduation" through which adults confirm adolescents and enjoin them to become responsible members of the adult society. Neither type of ritual adds a wholly new ritual element to the four already identified. Instead, they use all four previous ritual elements to guide adolescents' search for an ideology or "world image" congruent with their emerging sense of identity. Such ideologies in turn provide answers to the problems that develop when we leave childhood behind and envisage ourselves in adult roles. While these ideologies sometimes give simplistic answers to problems, they usually utilize the core meanings of the numinous, judicial, dramatic, and formal ritual elements in the formation of a new set of convictions about the world and our place in it. The ritualization process also reinforces these convictions by making it possible for us to have significant encounters with adolescents and adults who share these convictions. Thus ritualization supports "solidarity of conviction." It reinforces the adolescent's emerging sense of "I" by fostering solidarity with other "I's" with whom one is able to identify.[32]

But ritual in this stage can be pushed to excess. Erikson calls it the excess of totalism, a "fanatic and exclusive preoccupation with what seems unquestionably ideal within a tight system of ideas."[33] He sees such totalism as a "partial regression to idolism," the ritual excess of stage 1, because it has the same tendency to see situations as "all or nothing." In totalism, there is no place for moderation, and compromise is considered a sellout of one's convictions.

In the special rituals and rites of the church this ritual element is reflected in confirmation ceremonies and in evangelistic services and other proselyting activities designed to convert youth. We could evaluate these ritual forms in terms of how well they contribute to the youth's need for a sense of "I," the need of the adolescent and the church for solidarity of conviction, and the need to avoid totalism in fundamental matters of faith.[34] But we are concerned here with the ritualization of everyday church life. This draws our attention to how the congregation as a community of faith develops and maintains its convictional posture. An important feature of congregational life in this connection is its study and prayer groups. Whether they are primarily devoted to prayer, Bible study, or study of selected topical issues, the overall effect of these groups is to help form the congregation's convictional posture. The pastor's task as ritual coordinator is to assist the efforts of these groups, especially as they bear on the congregation's convictional posture or sense of Christian identity. The pastor's major concern is to help ensure that these study and prayer groups do not foster confusion about this convictional posture. Each study and prayer group is accountable to the congregation as a whole and should understand its role to be that of contributing to the congregation's quest for solidarity of conviction.

These study and prayer groups are vulnerable to the ritual excess of totalism, which happens when they become exclusive in membership or confuse uniformity of viewpoint with solidarity of conviction. Strategies for avoiding such totalism will vary with each congregation, but a major task of the pastor is to see that there are appropriate safeguards against this danger of totalism. The goal here is not conformity or even unanimity, but "solidarity." With the emergence of the Solidarity labor movement in Poland, we should not have too much difficulty visualizing what Erikson means by "solidarity of conviction." But I also find helpful an analogy closer to home and equally poignant. This is the kind of solidarity that family and friends, whatever their personal differences in the past, experience at the graveside ceremony on the occasion of the death of a loved one. Solidarity of conviction has the same sense of "standing together" in a context of "shared meanings." And like the grieving family, the congregation that enjoys such solidarity finds it an invaluable resource for maintaining their sense of orientation in the world.

The Affiliative Element (Young Adulthood)

Erikson describes the affiliative element in young adulthood as "encounters" between young adults who are bound together in "work, friendship, and love." The ritual excess here is the elitism which often pervades the conversations and actions of young adults and which is reflected in their "demonstrative display of shared tastes and predilections, of enthusiastic opinions and scathing judgments."[35]

In the life of the church this ritual element is manifest in the special rite of marriage. But in the everyday ritualization of the church's life, it is perhaps best reflected in friendships among church members and in the tendency of congregations to be family-oriented.

Friendship is an important aspect of the church's life, but much of the pastor's role in this regard involves seeing that friendships and cliques do not undermine the church's sense of being bound together in work and love. This means being especially aware of the danger of elitism among friendship groups in the church and taking initiatives when this elitism either causes other members to feel left out (stage 1), or impedes the congregation's efforts to make visitors and new members feel at home (stage 2), or causes other members to want to withdraw from certain involvements in the church (stage 3), or weakens the church's sense of discipline (stage 4), or threatens its solidarity of conviction (stage 5).

Another aspect of the affiliative element in church life is its family orientation. In contrast to most social organizations the church includes every age group from infants to the very old, and thus exemplifies the succession of generations. An important task of the pastor is to help coordinate the affiliative activities of the families, ensuring that the church is one place in contemporary society where families can "do things together." But because congregational life is family-oriented, the elitism that develops is often a family-oriented elitism. Whole families may feel left out or ostracized. Furthermore, adults who are not part of any family, adults who attend church without their spouse, and single-parent families are especially likely to be victims of this elitism.

Most pastors are fully aware of how the church's friendship groups and family orientation can have divisive, demoralizing effects. But this problem has become acute in recent years. More and more persons are leaving the church or maintaining minimal levels of commitment because they do not fit into the church's affiliative structure. Also, among persons who would normally fit into the church's affiliative structure there are those who are leaving, or maintaining low levels of commitment, because they are concerned that the affiliative structure of the church excludes persons and groups they would like to see included. Pastors are being called on to work more creatively with the congregation's "marginal" persons, not only because they represent a growing minority, but also because a church's effectiveness in ministering to its marginal constituency is perhaps the best single indicator of its vitality as a truly caring community. The nature of the core and marginal groups will differ from congregation to congregation; for example, it is not always the same age group that is marginal. But every congregation has such core and marginal groups, and they represent two different "ritual" styles reflecting different attitudes toward the church's dominant affiliative structure. As ritual coordinator the pastor participates in both ritual "worlds" and is often called on to interpret the ritual behavior of the one group to the other group.

The Generational Element (Adulthood)

By "generational" Erikson means that the adult assumes the responsibility of the ritualizer—the person who "conducts" the ritualization process. As the society's conductors of its ritual process adults must be willing to become the numinous model in the eyes of the next generation (stage 1), act as judge of good and evil (stage 2), transmit ideal values (stage 3), share knowledge of proven techniques (stage 4), and sanction the convictions and affiliations of adolescents and young adults (stages 5 and 6). This involves assuming an authoritative position, communicating the sense that "I know what I am doing," and is especially reflected in the adults' need to teach their young:

> Man needs to teach, not only for the sake of those who need to be taught, and not only for the fulfillment of his identity, but because facts are kept alive by being told, logic by being demonstrated, truth by being professed.[36]

By assuming the role of teacher the adult not only transmits truth but also overcomes the basic psychosocial problem of this period in life—the tendency toward stagnation and self-absorption.

The ritual excess of this stage is authoritism, the spurious exercise of authority. Authoritism is a serious problem for the ritualization process as a whole, because under its influence the young are susceptible to the ritual excesses of all the other stages of the process: idolism, legalism, impersonation and moralism, formalism, totalism, and elitism. Authoritism creates a social climate in which ritual excess has opportunity to flourish.

There is no special ritual or rite associated with the generational ritual element in the life of the church, unless we were to cite the

commissioning of church-school teachers and other leaders responsible for the care of the young (such as high-school youth directors
and sponsors). Indeed, every special rite identified thus far (from
baptism to marriage ceremonies) has a generational purpose, and
each is presided over by generational adults. Thus all the special
rituals conducted in the church are under the auspices of the generational ritual element, and the pastor's own formal ritual role is
essentially generational. (This is frequently a problem for younger
pastors who do not yet identify personally with the generational
role.)

Our main concern, though, is the ritualization of everyday church
life. We should center here on the church's responsibility to be a
"caring community." To clarify what this entails, the parables of
Jesus are especially illuminating. While they were not intended to
serve as moral examples of human caring, many parables suggest
that acts of human care are metaphors of God's activity in the world.
Through stories on the caring role of parents (Prodigal Son), care
of persons outside one's familiar group (Good Samaritan), care of
cherished traditions (Wedding Guests), and care of one's own soul
(Rich Fool), Jesus provides a screen through which we glimpse a
caring God. By portraying the costs, risks, and moral ambiguities of
caring, these parables also enable us to envision the caring community as itself a parable of Jesus—whose own caring bordered on the
irrational.

This view of the church as a caring community gives ultimate
purpose to the dramatic and ideological ritual elements, for Erikson's ritual schema invites us to orient personal involvement and
solidarity of conviction around the image of the caring community.
The kinds of care that a given congregation may provide depend on
local circumstances but Jesus' parables capture the atmosphere or
climate in which the caring community works. The Hidden Treas-
ures and Lost Coin parables invite us to imagine the nearly
unimaginable—that the caring community will abandon itself to an
uncertain future, or turn its own house upside down, in an all-
consuming desire to participate in God's care for the world. The
caring community would function in an eschatological atmosphere
of imminent danger and joyous self-abandon.

The Integral Element (Mature Adulthood)

Erikson notes how, in traditional societies, older persons validate the society's ritualization process by "personifying" the life this process is intended to foster. They may be wise persons themselves—we often associate wisdom with the old—but their major contribution is to exemplify the wisdom of the ritualization process itself. Younger persons can look at the old persons in their society and determine whether the process that made these older persons what they are is a process worthy of their own commitment and loyalty.

In *Toys and Reasons* Erikson calls the ritual excess of this stage "sapientism" or "the unwise pretense of being wise."[37] In *The Life Cycle Completed* he calls the ritualistic danger of this stage "dogmatism," "a compulsive pseudointegrity that, where linked to undue power, can become coercive orthodoxy."[38] In contrast, genuine wisdom in the old is a "simple integrity"[39] or "integrality"[40] that has no need of pretense or dogmatic reinforcement. In its simplest meaning it is a "tendency to keep things together" and "to have our wits about us" in spite of significant

> loss of linkages in all three organizing processes: in the Soma, the pervasive weakening of tonic interplay in connecting tissues, blood-distributing vessels, and the muscle system; in the Psyche, the gradual loss of mnemonic coherence in experience, past and present; and in the Ethos, the threat of a sudden and nearly total loss of responsible function in generative interplay.[41]

This tendency to keep things together is not some "rare quality of personal character" but "a proclivity for understanding . . . the integrative ways of human life."[42]

In the congregational setting we have no special rituals or rites that reflect this ritual element. Also no single aspect of the church's everyday ritualization personifies the ritual wisdom of the congregation. This is because the integral element is concerned with the church's whole ritualization process. It concerns the overall integrity of that process, its contribution to wholeness of life in the congregation. While some older adults in the congregation may be especially good exemplars of this ritual wisdom, such wisdom should be more broadly evident in the general ethos of the community. Participants ought to be able to sense that this congregation "personifies" wisdom, that the church as a whole is an exemplar of the wisdom of its ritualization processes.

The dangers here are sapientism and dogmatism which, like the sapientism and dogmatism of older adults, may be due to various causes. A congregation's pretense of being wise, or its compulsive pseudointegrity, may be an attempt to disguise apathy, as reflected in a reluctance to acquire new knowledge and a reliance on old, outmoded facts and procedures. It may be due to deep frustration and despair, as reflected in an effort to maintain an image of wholeness in the face of gradual but irrevocable disintegration and helplessness. It may hide a silent contempt or disgust for what the church has become in recent years or have its roots in a glorification of the church's past when the congregation and its pastors were presumably imbued with uncommon wisdom. It might be due to the larger religious ethos in which the congregation finds itself, where the congregation can pretend to personify wisdom because other churches seem patently lacking in this quality. Or it may be due to the church having undue power (such as wealth and prestige) that permits it to resort to coercive dogmatism. These few examples suggest that there may be rather close parallels between the causes of sapientism and dogmatism in old age and similar forms of pseudointegrity in a congregational community.

Granted that sapientism and dogmatism are relatively easy to discover in the church, what about wisdom? What is it that enables us to say that a given congregation is the very "personification of ritual wisdom"? The congregation that personifies ritual wisdom is one which reflects on the meaning and purpose of its ritualization processes. Freud complained that rituals are enacted for reasons that are no longer remembered much less understood by the ritualizers. It is important for a congregation to develop this understanding by engaging in continuing reflection on its ritual processes. Because it consists so much of repeated activities the ritualization process helps the congregation to order its life and to orient itself to the world in which it finds itself. But this process can also become the cause of disorder, disorientation, or pseudo-orientation if we do not reflect on its meaning and purpose, especially in the light of changing circumstances within the congregation (its Soma and Psyche) and in the world around us (the Ethos). An important task of the pastor as ritual coordinator—perhaps the most important task because the most integrative—is to lead the congregation in reflecting on its ritual processes.

Healthy and Unhealthy Church Communities

Because constructive ritualization is vital to the social health of a community—whereas ritual excesses lead to social pathology—the foregoing analysis of the church's ritual process enables us to identify characteristics of healthy and unhealthy church communities. Eight such characteristics will be mentioned here.

1. In the healthy church every person's *distinctiveness is recognized and confirmed.* Efforts are made by the pastor to identify the special qualities and interests of each member. Often, special efforts are made to ensure that newer members have an opportunity to discover and express their distinctive abilities. Recognizing the distinctiveness of one another is not just "good psychology." It is one vital means afforded the community to actualize its life in God for, as we have seen, it is in the nature of God to recognize us as distinctive persons, and it is the role of the church to confirm this divine recognition through its special rites of baptism, communion, and funeral. In the unhealthy church recognition becomes a matter of mutual manipulation and members (including the pastor) are therefore immobilized when it is not always forthcoming.

2. In the healthy church there are well-established and commonly understood (though not necessarily highly formal) *procedures for expressing disapproval.* Disapproval is handled in such a manner as to avoid unnecessary shaming. Members of the congregation (including the pastor) may suffer criticism or defeat, but never are they stripped of their essential dignity. Protracted trials are avoided because dragging out the process makes it possible for extraneous issues to be introduced into the conflict or dispute. In the unhealthy church there is much false contrition and frequent arbitrary tests of compliance with church rules and regulations.

3. In the healthy church all members are involved in roles that reflect the convergence of their sense of "I" and the Christian story.

The healthy church provides a microreality through which its individual members relive, create, and re-create past experiences and anticipate future roles. The healthy church also provides many occasions for constructive reminiscence on its own immediate and distant past, and for rehearsal of its immediate and more distant future. The unhealthy church does not provide such occasions. Moreover, unlike the healthy church it does not test its internal drama against external realities. In a sense, the unhealthy church creates for itself a make-believe world.

4. In the healthy church, members *communicate with one another in an open but disciplined way.* Their communication is not formalistic, but it does pay attention to the fact that serious misunderstandings are caused by inaccurate communication of feelings and intentions. The healthy church recognizes that many internal problems are the result of undisciplined communication, of double messages, for example. The healthy church also recognizes that "uneventful speech" or "vacuous communication" can be demoralizing both for those who must listen to it and for those doing the talking. In the unhealthy church the members lack discipline in communicating with one another. They use language in arbitrary, unpredictable ways, often in ways that support moralistic coercion. No matter what may be the educational level of the membership, such churches are functionally illiterate.

5. The healthy church is not a collection of individuals but a *community of shared experiences and meanings.* The healthy church has developed a sense of solidarity that goes deeper than personality differences and interpersonal conflicts. This solidarity is based not on exclusion of or antagonism toward outgroups, but on shared convictions about the community's orientation *in* the world. In most churches, these convictions are tacit ones, not necessarily raised to full consciousness. They are often discernible by outsiders, however. The unhealthy church is a collection of individuals who lack or do not acknowledge shared experience and meanings. Alternatively, the unhealthy church achieves its sense of community through a tight and rigid system of ideas and customs, where there is no place for moderation, innovation, and compromise. Such churches are totalistic, and are often under the sway of adult authoritism.

6. The healthy church *opens itself to others, resisting the impulse to withdraw into itself*. It achieves this, in part, through its internal openness reflected in a resistance within its own membership to elitism based on age, gender, economic status, or ethnic heritage. It fosters constructive friendships across age and gender lines, and does not allow members to engage in systematic discrimination against one or another of its own constituencies. In contrast the unhealthy church is closed to outsiders and it engages in various forms of elitism within the church community itself. Often one constituent group enjoys higher status than others, and the resources of the community are typically directed toward this group's interests to the exclusion of the interests of other groups.

7. The healthy church is essentially a *caring community*. The adult members of the church recognize that their primary responsibility is to create an atmosphere of caring, and to instill in the children and youth a passion and capacities for caring. If anything defines a church as genuinely Christian, it is the church's capacity to care in joyful self-abandon and, as required, at personal risk. In contrast, the unhealthy church is uncaring. This does not necessarily mean that it is openly callous. Rather, it is apathetic, unmoved by the needs and desires of others. The unhealthy church finds it difficult—hard work—to generate caring actions or responses to others. Once this apathy gets its deadly grip on a church, it is extremely difficult to alter that church's course toward total disorientation, because apathy leaves the church susceptible to ritual excesses of every kind.

8. The healthy church does not take its essential integrity or integrality for granted but *continues to reflect on what it is about in light of changing internal and external circumstances.* It does not wait for crises in order to engage in this reflection; it engages in such reflection on a continuing basis. The healthy church wants to have its wits about it, and therefore takes seriously the task of evaluating its ritual processes in the light of changing circumstances. The unhealthy church is rather unreflective about itself. It maintains its customary ritual processes on the grounds that it has always done things this way, or such-and-such a group insists that it be done this way. The unhealthy church congratulates itself on maintaining its traditions, even if this proves to be a kind of pseudowisdom, a failure to make essential

adaptations to changing circumstances. The fate of the insect is instructive here. The insect is a species that resisted change and instead became more and more sophisticated within a diminished sphere of influence. What appeared to be increasing refinement of skills was actually a form of social pathology, a parody (not personification) of ritual wisdom.[43]

Given the fact that church and family dynamics are often similar, and that both are essentially caring communities, the foregoing points are also applicable to the healthy and unhealthy family. It should also be stressed that, concerning churches and families, the terms "healthy" and "unhealthy" are ideal types. In reality, churches and families fall somewhere between the two extreme poles of perfect health and total pathology.

Ritual and Faith Maintenance

When pastoral care of the church is viewed in ritualization terms, we see that its major concern is to help persons acquire and maintain a sense of being oriented in the world. This means that pastoral care is concerned with basic issues of faith. Faith means having an orientation in the world, a perspective from which to experience the world and interpret this experience. The ritualization of everyday church life helps persons maintain this orientation. As noted in chapter 1, the major causes of disorientation are moral confusion, pain, and the sense that our lives fail to hold together in a meaningful, comprehensible way. Pastoral care is appropriately concerned with all three causes of disorientation, but pastoral care through the church's everyday ritualization process is especially directed toward the third cause. How to hold our lives together in a meaningful, comprehensible way (that is, in a way that takes seriously the formlessness of much contemporary life) is precisely the problem that ritualization of everyday church life dramatizes and addresses.

Mircea Eliade tells the story of a primitive tribe whose communal life was centered around a sacred pole. When the tribe traveled, the pole would go with them and wherever they settled, it was placed at the center of their encampment. The pole was their means of being oriented in the world, making it comprehensible to them. But one morning they awoke and found the pole broken in half. They wandered around in confusion and finally lay down on the ground and waited to die.[44] This story illustrates how ritual helps us to maintain our orientation in the world and how it is essential to maintaining solidarity of conviction, or faith. When deprived of their primary means of ritualizing their experience, the tribe became thoroughly disoriented. When ritual fails, the people lose faith.

In chapter 5 I will draw connections between Erikson's theory of ritual and the Book of Proverbs for the purpose of developing a new model of pastoral care. Like Erikson, Proverbs recognizes the importance of the ritualization of everyday life. Unlike the priestly tradition, which was responsible for conducting special rites and holy days, the proverbial tradition in ancient Israel was concerned with the ritualization of the everyday life of the community. It viewed this ritualization as a means of maintaining a way of life that holds people, individually and collectively, together. Because it is concerned with this basic function of ritual, Proverbs is a vital biblical resource for pastoral care.

CHAPTER 4

The Personal Comforter

Suffering is a major cause of disorientation in the world. It can be caused by physical, psychological, or social factors. But whatever its source, suffering affects the total person and causes us to perceive the world as an inhospitable, if not downright hostile, place to be. Persons who have been pushed to the limits of their capacity to endure pain have often begged for release from this world. Persons who have watched the suffering of another have been so pained by the experience that they have been driven to kill the other, or themselves. Death, though it means relinquishing our claim on the world, can seem infinitely more desirable than continuing to live in such excruciating pain.

This chapter focuses on shame, a form of pain that directs our attention to the disorienting effects of pain and challenges us to deepen our understanding of the pastor's role as personal comforter. Shame has a psychological cause, so its painfulness is often less observable than severe forms of physical pain. Moreover, shame is a type of painful experience that we desperately want to disguise from others, so it becomes a peculiarly private form of suffering. But this only underscores how disorienting shame can be. Together with doubt shame is the negative pole of the second stage of the life cycle. Thus shame is the first major threat to the growing child's newly won sense of being "at home" in the world. And throughout life shame continues to threaten our sense that we can be at peace in the world.

This chapter is only an initial step toward a more complete analysis of the problem of shame from a pastoral care perspective. It does not go much beyond laying the foundations for an understanding of shame that is theologically and pastorally responsible. However, it does recognize that such an understanding of shame needs to take account of two fundamental facts. The first is that pain has played a central role in the Christian faith since the Crucifixion, and while shame is not the only pain associated with the Crucifixion, it is certainly one of the most prominent. The second is that our contemporary society places heavy emphasis on pain avoidance; it is especially keen on avoiding shame. Thus there is a basic conflict between traditional Christianity and contemporary society in their attitudes toward shame, and this conflict must be taken seriously in any effort to think theologically about our pastoral response to the experience of shame.

THREE CHARACTERISTICS
OF SHAME

Shame is a common experience, and in the vast majority of cases it is a painful experience. It is not an experience we seek, and it is an experience we want to forget. But just what is shame? In *On Shame and the Search for Identity* Helen Merrell Lynd identifies the major characteristics of shame. I will discuss them under three headings: the phenomenological experience of shame, the personal effects of shame, and the effect of shame on our world view.[1]

The Phenomenological Experience of Shame

How does shame feel to the person who is experiencing it? In the first place one feels exposed. A common reaction to shame is that we have been exposed to the view of others. Shame is often described as feeling that "everyone was looking at me" or wishing it were possible to "sink through the floor." But being exposed to others is only part of the experience of shame. There is also self-exposure. Shame forces us to "see" ourselves. It makes us conscious of ourselves— "self-conscious." Normally, we can go about our lives without much self-awareness, but the experience of shame suddenly forces us to be aware of ourselves. And, invariably, the self that shame reveals to us is one we would prefer not to see. Lynd concludes that "the exposure to oneself is at the heart of shame."[2] Also, the feeling of being exposed to other people is not necessarily limited to those who are literally present. Sometimes we are alone but experience shame because we feel "watched." The "watchers" may be other persons, such as parents or old friends, who would be "horrified" if they could see what we are doing now. Or the watcher may be God, from whom no secrets are hidden.

Typically, this exposure through shame is thoroughly unexpected. In guilt experiences that is not necessarily true: choice, foresight, and awareness of what one is planning to do are all possible. As the legal language has it guilty acts may be "premeditated." This is not the case with shame. In shame we have no prior warning, and we may not even realize until the experience is over that we have just felt shame. Frequently, the reaction to shame is: "If I had known this would happen, I wouldn't have put myself in this situation"—I would not have volunteered in class, gone to the party, put my name in for the new job opening. But this is just the point: shame is an experience that we cannot anticipate in advance. That is why people experiencing shame wish they were dreaming. They cannot believe it is happening because they had no prior warning. Also, most experiences of shame happen in a moment. They are not of long duration but are over virtually before they begin. The offensive end drops the quarterback's perfect pass in the end zone before a crowd of 80,000 spectators and millions of home "viewers," and the deed is done. There is no opportunity to anticipate the experience and no way to adjust oneself to it. The full impact of exposure is felt at once. The exposure of shame is immediate and complete.

Besides the feeling of exposure there is the sense that the whole experience is inappropriate or incongruous. The experience of shame feels out of place, as though an element of absurdity has been injected into a normal and ordinary state of affairs. Persons who experience shame and then try to tell someone about it often begin with "I know it sounds trivial . . ." or "It's silly, really, but. . . ." Yet for all its seeming triviality, this experience may exert far greater influence on our lives than truly important events. We may have difficulty remembering how and when we learned a profound insight about the world we live in, yet remember to the minutest detail an occasion when we were tongue-tied. Or we may go on to become accomplished in our work and yet not be able to banish from our mind the time when a grade-school teacher said, loud enough for the whole class to hear, "I expected you to do much better on this test." Shame experiences are anomalies, and while we cannot deny that they are part of our experience, they seem alien to it. In fact, the same experience can happen to other persons and not cause them to feel shame at all. The friend who says, "Don't worry about it—I forget my lines every year and it's no big deal" is small comfort to the child who is agonizing over the evening's failure. Shame's incongruity results not from the objective event itself but from the fact that it is incongruous *for this individual.*

The Personal Effects of Shame

What effect does shame have on us as persons? Lynd suggests that in the first place shame is a threat to trust. To experience shame is to find that one's trust in the world is not always warranted. Our expectations of how the world functions or hangs together are violated. We discover that we trusted ourselves to a situation that was not really there. When we enter the room and find that everyone is dressed other than we expected or when we believe we have the right answer and respond confidently to the teacher's question only to be told we are wrong, the situation we thought was there proves an illusion. We ourselves are still there, but the anticipated context is not.

Jesus' parable of the rich fool is pertinent here. Contrary to much popular opinion this parable is not about greed but about misperception of the situation.[3] The rich fool thought his situation was secure, that it certainly merited trust. The barns were full and the future looked promising. But this was not the situation at all. This was the day appointed for him to die! He had trusted himself to a situation that was not there. In a similar way experiences of shame from time to time bring us to a vivid, unpleasant awareness that we have misperceived our real situation. In life cycle terms the shame experienced in stage 2 is an assault on the basic trust established in stage 1. The plaintive cry of shame—"If only someone had reached out and spared me from falling on my face"—is an expression of longing for the trustworthy environment one came to expect in stage 1. We can endure a few assaults on our basic sense of trust. But many such experiences, or a few especially devastating ones, can lead to mistrust of virtually every situation we encounter. Then we anticipate that the arms will not reach out to save us, and we even wonder if the floor will sustain us. Freud has said that the ultimate assurance is that "we cannot fall out of this world."[4] Since shame is often associated with the feeling of sinking through the floor, severe experiences of shame threaten this fundamental assurance. This is why we associate shame with "fallenness." And this is why shame experiences cause us to be a little less trusting and a little more cautious and calculating the next time around.

A second effect of shame is that it is totally self-involving. Lynd distinguishes between guilty actions which we *do,* and shameful experiences which we *are.* An act of wrongdoing, even one of serious consequences, need not undermine our sense of who we are because we can explain or rationalize the action as not characteristic of us. In this way guilt is externalized. But shame involves our whole self and cannot be externalized. As Lynd points out, shame experiences involve exposure to "peculiarly sensitive, intimate, vulnerable aspects of the self."[5] Because in shame we have a heightened sensitivity to our self, Lynd sees a direct connection between shame and identity. The central task in finding one's identity is to acquire a sense of "I" or a coherent sense of self. When we experience shame we ask, "Was that really me?" We want to dissociate ourselves from the "self" revealed in shame. Among the many selves that may be incorporated into our sense of "I," those identified with shame are ones we generally want to repudiate. Our "shameful self" is most likely to be relegated to our "negative identity."

Attempts to dissociate ourselves from our shameful self usually take one of three forms. The first and most common is to ignore our shameful self as being unimportant. We focus our attention instead on our more positive and satisfying selves and tell ourselves that our shameful self is insignificant. The experience of shame itself lends support to this view, because many shame experiences are incongruous and inappropriate. Since our shameful self became evident to us through seemingly trivial experiences, we conclude that it has no relevance to our emerging identity.

The second approach is to recognize that our shameful self is an important part of us but to renounce it. In this case we acknowledge that it is part of who we are, but we are determined that it will not be part of our positive identity. Sometimes individuals renounce their shameful self through a religious conversion.

The third approach is to continue to engage in experiences that originally led us to experience shame but at the same time seek to eliminate feelings of shame from these experiences. The hope is that in time we can dissociate shame from experiences that we do not or cannot renounce (for example, sexual experiences).

All three approaches are unsatisfactory as a response to the problem of our shameful self. In one way or another they all counsel a denial of our shameful self. We need rather to take a diametrically opposite view of this self that is disclosed to us through the experience of shame. From a Christian point of view the shameful self is neither peripheral nor expendable but is absolutely central to our identity. In a moment I will discuss this alternative view of the shameful self.

The Effect of Shame on Our World View

Shame can also have a powerful effect on our world view. In the first place, it brings us in touch with tragedy, especially the tragic dimensions of the relationships between generations. For parents this often happens when their children are adolescents or young adults and have become pregnant out of wedlock, gotten fired from a job, engaged in criminal activities, become involved in a line of work that offends the parents' sense of dignity and worth, lived in a manner that violates the parents' own moral code, or developed severe emotional problems. Parents also cause their children shame at various stages in life. In adolescence children may become ashamed of their parents' life style and thus develop a reluctance to invite friends into their home. Later, as adults, they may become ashamed of their aging parents because of the older ones' physical or mental condition. Prov. 23:22 addresses this shame: "Hearken to your father who begot you, and do not despise your mother when she is old."

A tragic example of shame felt for a parent is given in Elie Wiesel's account of the death of his father when they were imprisoned at Buchenwald during World War II. Wiesel was fifteen years old at the time and fighting for his own survival. His father was nearly dead from exhaustion and starvation. Wiesel tells how his father became the object of derision and hostility from other inmates because he was "unable to drag himself outside to relieve himself." Then his father died one night. When Elie discovered in the morning that his father's bed had been assigned to another invalid, he could not weep: "It pained me that I could not weep. But I had no more tears. And, in the depths of my being, in the recesses of my weakened conscience, could I have searched it, I might have perhaps found something like—free at last!"[6]

In this episode the tragic nature of life is revealed through the experience of shame. Wiesel felt shame for his father as the older man suffered insult and abuse. His father's humiliation was "a wound to the heart" and "another reason for living lost." But then Wiesel's shame turned back on himself; his only response to his father's death was the sense that a burden had been lifted: "free at last!" This was the shame of a son who could not weep at his father's death but instead felt genuine relief. This is an extreme example of the tragic sense of life. But it points to the fact that whenever shame plays a role in the relations between generations it is likely to be a tragic role. As Lynd points out, "The impact of shame for others may reach even deeper than shame for ourselves."[7]

The second effect of shame on our world view is to make us aware of the difficulty of human communication. Shameful experiences are hard to talk about; they are also hard to listen to.

They are difficult to talk about because, when we tell the story as it really happened, we reexperience the shame and the pain that goes along with it. So we leave crucial details out, and when we do this, we fail to gain the relief we sought in the first place. There is also the problem that the persons to whom we tell the story often consider it trivial and treat it as unimportant. One incongruous feature of shame is that feelings so deep can be experienced in events so seemingly trivial. When we relate the experience to other persons, they often pick up on this incongruity and suggest that we should not feel the experience as deeply and painfully as we do.

Shame experiences are also difficult to listen to if they are told fully and heard for what they are. Often this is because other persons would rather not be drawn into our private life. The same exposure that was painful for us when the event occurred is painful for others when we expose them to this recounting.

The effect of these communication difficulties is that shame experiences isolate us from other people. They isolate us when they occur, and they isolate us when we relate them to others. Thus shame often makes us feel alone in the world. There is some aspect of our lives that will never be known to others, a deep pain that others, no matter how sympathetic, cannot feel. As Paul Pruyser points out:

> We must . . . take into consideration the utter subjectivity of pain, on account of which people in pain cannot automatically rely on recognition, let alone legitimation, of their condition by others. . . . Pain-as-felt stands in some tension to objective criteria by which outsiders seek to validate it.[8]

SHAME AS INJURY TO SELF

What is the pain we experience in shame? Lynd's emphasis on the total involvement of the self in shame provides the answer. We experience pain because we have sustained an injury to self. Shame is an assault on our dignity because it makes us feel humiliated or embarrassed, and it results in loss of self-esteem or positive self-regard because it makes us feel ashamed of ourselves.

Our first reaction to this inflicting of injury on self is to seek escape (make a quick exit, make ourselves invisible, convince ourselves it's all a dream). When escape proves impossible we try other alternatives. We may defend our injured self through anger, putting the blame on others for getting us into this painful situation or for failing to prepare us adequately for it, or becoming angry with ourselves for getting involved in something we should have avoided. Blaming ourselves or others for this self-injury may be a useful coping mechanism. But this is hardly an adequate interpretation of the experience. There is more at stake than assigning blame. As David Bakan points out, pain insists that its meaning be probed:

> To attempt to understand the nature of pain, to seek to find its meaning, is already to respond to an imperative of pain itself. No experience demands and insists upon interpretation in the same way. Pain forces the question of its meaning, and especially of its cause, insofar as cause is an important part of its meaning.[9]

We need to discover for ourselves what shame experiences mean—their significance for who we are as persons and for how we understand our situation in the world.

SHAME AND CHRISTIAN IDENTITY

This brings us back to the three approaches to shame noted a moment ago under "Personal Effects," and sets the stage for an alternative approach which I consider to be more fundamentally Christian. These three approaches are attempts to interpret the experience of shame and to understand what it entails for one's identity. But in each of the three we try to dissociate ourselves from the pain of shame, from the injury that shame does to our sense of "I." These three approaches are based on pain avoidance. The interpretation of shame that I propose is diametrically opposed to this. I suggest that the painful experience of shame is not to be avoided or renounced but instead made the core of our identity as Christians. Why the core of Christian identity? Because in shame we experience the pain of self-exposure, and the core of Christian identity is to be "exposed before God." The point of Christian identity is not to put our shameful self behind us but to allow it to be exposed, again and again, to God.

Shame and Self-Disclosure

Let us explore this interpretation of shame through *The Confessions of St. Augustine*[10] which reveals how Augustine found his identity as a Christian by exposing his shameful self to God. The *Confessions* have usually been viewed as reflecting a struggle with guilt. But Paul Pruyser's observation that "very little guilt feeling is expressed directly" in the *Confessions* should put us on guard.[11]

Perhaps the real feeling level for Augustine has instead to do with shame. Perhaps our tendency to view this book as solely an account of guilt is an illustration of how shame is so hard to communicate. Modern readers expect "confessions" to take the form of guilt, so when Augustine talks of shame they fail to hear him.

I will not try to document my thesis that the *Confessions* is more about shame than guilt. One brief illustration will have to suffice, namely, Augustine's account of the death of a friend. Augustine had just begun his teaching career in his native town. He was about nineteen or twenty years old. The friend, whom he had known from childhood, contracted a fever and lay for many days in an unconscious state. When it appeared certain he would die, he was baptized a Christian. But he rallied temporarily and, during the time that he was still lucid, Augustine tried to joke with him about his Christian baptism. These jokes were not appreciated by his friend. Augustine says that "he was horrified at me as if I were an enemy, and he warned me with a swift and admirable freedom that if I wished to remain his friend, I must stop saying such things to him. I was struck dumb and was disturbed, but I concealed all my feelings until he would grow well again and would be fit in health and strength."[12] But the friend did not get well. After a few days he suffered a relapse and died.

Augustine's reflections on this episode center on his grief and sorrow over the death of his friend. He says that his native town and his father's house became a "torment" to him in the absence of his friend. But he also reproaches himself for making fun of his friend's baptism. His jokes about the baptism come back to haunt him, and he is profoundly ashamed of his behavior. Now, he says to God, "I do not blush to confess your mercies to me and to call upon you, I who once did not blush to profess before men all my blasphemies and to bark like a dog against you."[13]

Apart from this reference to blushing, Augustine does not use the language of shame to convey his deep sense of self-reproach for the way he treated his dying friend. Yet this is a situation in which shame, not guilt, is clearly the dominant emotion. As we have seen, one major source of shame is the sense that one's words or actions have been incongruous or inappropriate, and this is precisely how Augustine now views his attempt to joke about his friend's baptism. Lynd writes:

> It is peculiarly characteristic of these situations of suddenly experienced incongruity or discrepancy that evoke shame that they are often occasioned by what seems a "ridiculously" slight incident. An ostensibly trivial incident has precipitated intense emotion. . . . It is the very triviality of the cause—an awkward gesture . . . an untimely joke . . . a witticism that falls flat . . . that helps to give shame its unbearable character.[14]

Augustine felt humiliated when his friend rebuked him for his untimely joke. But the greatest shame is what he experiences now as he opens this shameful deed to God's scrutiny and judgment.

What are we to make of Augustine's account of his experience of shame? What do such experiences mean for Christian identity? The answer is provided by Augustine himself as he reflects on what he has disclosed to God in the earlier pages of his *Confessions.* He writes in his chapter entitled "A Philosophy of Memory":

> Lord, before whose eyes the abyss of man's conscience lies naked, what thing within me could be hidden from you, even if I would not confess it to you? I would be hiding you from myself, not myself from you. But now, since my groans bear witness that I am a thing displeasing to myself, you shine forth, and you are pleasing to me, and you are loved and longed for, so that I may feel shame for myself . . . and choose you.[15]

Note especially the sentence "I would be hiding you from myself, not myself from you." By trying to avoid his shame, the awful sense of being exposed, Augustine realized that he would not be hiding from God but hiding God from himself. This is why it was so essential for him to focus on his shameful experiences and probe their meaning, even though this was painful for him to do. The issue for Augustine is no longer Adam's question, "How can I conceal my shame?" The question now is, "How may God become known to me?" And the answer is that as we cross the boundary from avoiding shame to embracing it, accepting it as the most intimate part of ourselves, we create the inner climate in which God becomes revealed to us.

What Augustine has done in the *Confessions* is to make the "self" of which we are most profoundly ashamed the very core of our Christian identity. Throughout the book he centers his attention and analytic insights on experiences which reveal his shameful self. Some of the experiences he recounts (such as a pear-stealing episode during adolescence) seem rather trivial. But this is because they are shame experiences, and many shame experiences do seem trivial and inconsequential. What all of Augustine's shame experiences have in common is the fact that they expose his shameful self and give rise to the pain that accompanies such exposure. These experiences were undoubtedly painful when he first experienced them. They are clearly painful to recall to memory now. Thus it often takes him a long time to begin relating these incidents, as the details come out in bits and pieces. But he needs to recount them, in spite of the pain, because he knows that as he exposes his shameful self, God is being revealed to him.

What is the basis for the claim that one comes to know God through disclosure of one's own shame? Thoughtful Christians like Augustine are led to this conviction because the death of Jesus was by all accounts a shameful experience. Crucified as a common criminal in full public view, Jesus experienced shame of the most excruciating kind. Its injury to self was incalculable. Thus to view life from the perspective of the cross, as Christians do, is to embrace our shameful selves, for Jesus' experience on the cross is the paradigmatic shame experience for Christians. For him the cross entailed self-exposure and incongruity, threat to trust and total self-involvement, tragedy and isolation.

To put our shameful selves aside is to dissociate ourselves experientially from the shame of the cross. On the other hand, to embrace our shameful self is to identify with Jesus and thereby experience God as no longer hidden. As Erikson points out in *Young Man Luther,* Luther saw that "the passion is all that man can know of God; his conflicts, duly faced, are all that he can know of himself."[16]

The Method of Self-Disclosure

Augustine's method for becoming familiar with his shameful self is also important; the *Confessions* are one long extended prayer. It is relatively easy to see why prayer would be the preferred method for probing our experiences of shame and exposing them to God's view. In prayer, especially solitary prayer, we enter into intimate conversation with God. In this conversational setting we are able to "tell the story" of our shameful experiences, including all details, and this is precisely what Augustine does throughout the *Confessions*. With God as our conversation partner we can tell the story without fear that it will be judged trivial or unimportant, because we are confident that the God who is known through the Passion understands the depth of our pain. As the story unfolds, we are able to probe its meaning without the reserve or self-censorship that occurs when we relate these experiences to another person. As Augustine puts it, "the abyss of man's conscience lies naked" before the eyes of God. So there is nothing to be gained from excluding certain aspects of the story or failing to probe every possible meaning of the experience for our self-understanding.

When such exploration of our experiences occurs in the atmosphere of prayer, we orient ourselves to God's own perspective on these experiences. Like communication between two people who have come to know each other exceedingly well and are therefore able to anticipate one another's perspective on any given issue or topic without verbal exchange, prayer allows us to anticipate God's own understanding of the experiences we recount, even though no words are spoken.[17] Thus exposing ourselves through prayer enables us to gain insight into God's own view of the experience. This is what Augustine means when he says that he would be hiding God from himself if he did not disclose his shame to God. In self-disclosive prayer, what is revealed to us of God is God's perspective on our self-disclosures.

Self-disclosive prayer is painful because it means reliving shameful experiences all over again. But prayer of this kind may also provide comfort, restoring our sense of being "at home" in the world. For to welcome these experiences into our consciousness is to begin making peace with them. When we no longer treat them as alien to ourselves, we become more at peace with ourselves. Furthermore, welcoming these experiences into our consciousness through prayer means that we perceive them from God's perspective—and experience them no longer as isolated selves.

THE PASTOR AS
PERSONAL COMFORTER

Shame is only one of a vast variety of experiences that cause pain. But given the importance of shame to Christian identity, knowledge of how the Christian faith views shame provides critical insights into the Christian orientation to all forms of pain.

Such knowledge also helps us better to understand the pastor's role as personal comforter. While not all implications of the preceding discussion of shame for this pastoral role can be explored, we can focus on what is the most important implication. This concerns the fact that shame is painful because it simultaneously exposes and isolates us. Thus pain reveals things about ourselves which we would prefer not to acknowledge (our weakness, vulnerability, or previous errors in judgment) and it creates barriers between ourselves and others (our inability to communicate what we are going through and their inability to understand and respond meaningfully). On the basis of our discussion of Augustine's *Confessions* we can say that the Christian response to these two effects of painful experiences is this: in coming to terms with pain, we need to intensify (not reduce or eliminate) our sense of exposure, for this is the only way we will be able to overcome our sense of isolation (which from a Christian point of view is the great tragedy of pain). Henri Nouwen has something like this response in mind when he says, "A minister is not a doctor whose primary task is to take away pain. Rather he deepens the pain to a level where it can be shared."[18]

Let us consider this Christian response to pain and its implications for pastoral care by reviewing a pastoral visit reported in Cryer and Vayhinger's *Casebook in Pastoral Counseling.*[19] In exploring this case I first want to establish that it concerns shame and thus reflects the dynamics of pain that we have been exploring here. Then I will comment on what this case has to tell us about the pastor's role as personal comforter.

To set the stage: Mrs. A, a 68-year-old woman, was dying of cancer. She had been a good church person and apparently her own minister was making regular pastoral visits. But one Sunday after

church, her son asked his own pastor to call. As will become clear she
seems to have wanted her son's pastor to visit her because she was
preparing to relate a shameful experience which she did not want
her own pastor to know about.

After the pastor entered her room and sat down, Mrs. A began: "I
suppose you know I'm going to die?" Their conversation continued
for a brief moment on how she would miss the beautiful things in
life, and then she began to focus on her concern:

MRS. A: You know, Reverend, lying in bed waiting to die has some
good points. I've been thinking. It's all so silly—I mean, life—its
arguments, feuds, and all. It's all so silly when you think about it.

PASTOR: It's easy to place the stress at the wrong point in life, I
suppose.

MRS. A: Oh, how true. Sometimes I feel like laughing at my life.
When I think of the heartaches and tears and . . . worries, I just
feel like laughing. It's . . . it's all so futile. Isn't it in the Bible,
"Vanity of vanities! All is vanity"?

The conversation shifted briefly to her awareness that she was dying
and then returned to her past life, "its arguments, feuds, and all."
Mrs. A says: "If we could only relive parts of our lives again," and the
pastor picks it up.

PASTOR: You feel there might have been times when you could
have been different?

MRS. A: Yes, I know you'll think it's silly, Reverend, but for a long
time I've been president of our ladies' group; almost twenty
years, I guess. And once, when the girls were going to consider
another president, I—I did a terrible thing. I let them think the
other woman was . . . not good enough. Now she's gone, poor
soul . . . and I keep thinking about it. It wasn't very Christian,
was it, Reverend?

PASTOR: Being a Christian is very difficult. It seems to me that we
are bound to fail once in a while. But that's the greatness of our
faith; there is always room for failures. Forgiveness is part of
God's nature.

MRS. A: (She looked back at me; she seemed tired) I guess we all sin
. . . at times; and I suppose forgiveness is ours.

The pastor at this point proposed prayer and recited the Lord's Prayer. When he finished she said, "Even the Lord's Prayer sounds different now." As he got up to go she added, "I hope I haven't bored you." He assured her that she had not.

Distinguishing Guilt and Shame

Guilt is the official "theology" of our churches, and we have ritualized means for addressing it (as in public and private confession). So it was natural for the pastor in this case to view Mrs. A's "confession" as a matter of guilt and to assure her that forgiveness was available. Most interpreters of this case agree with him, viewing it as a matter of guilt. Mrs. A told a lie and now, as she faces death, feels guilty about it. But there is also a strong element of shame involved. In fact, shame is the dominant emotion.

Shame is evident in Mrs. A's reference to the "silliness" of the matter. She suspects that the pastor will find her story trivial and betrays this suspicion when she says at the end of his visit, "I hope I haven't bored you." Shame is also a factor in her hesitancy to reveal the details of this experience. Of the woman she denigrated, Mrs. A says, "I told a lie about her," but does not reveal the nature of the lie. She merely says that she let the other women in the group think that the rival candidate was "not good enough," suggesting that she may have raised doubts about this woman's moral character.

Shame is also apparent in the fact that the "terrible thing" she did caused injury to her self-esteem. Like Augustine reflecting on his jokes about Christian baptism, Mrs. A's action is an offense to her perception of herself as a "good Christian." She is ashamed of herself for having resorted to lying about the other woman in order to retain the presidency. She takes little comfort in the fact that it was an impulsive, unpremeditated reaction to the threat of losing her position. She has had to live with this blot on her character ever since, with the injury to self that it has caused.

Shame is the major reason she has been "thinking about" this seemingly trivial episode, working it over in her mind as she anticipates the end of her days on this earth. Trying to think of the more beautiful things of this world she has found herself reflecting instead on this "silly" matter. In fact, this seemingly trivial episode threatens her belief that life has any real meaning. She feels like laughing at life's incongruities. Life seems "all so futile." The biblical passage that comes to mind is "Vanity of vanities! All is vanity!"

Mrs. A's "tired" and somewhat skeptical reaction to the pastor's assurance of forgiveness may also be due to his use of "guilt language" for a situation where shame was the dominant emotion. She seems to be feeling: "I know I can receive forgiveness for telling a lie. But what can I do about the shame I feel?" On the other hand, his recitation of the Lord's Prayer is apparently quite meaningful to her. This familiar prayer suddenly sounds "different." It may be that having disclosed her shameful act to the pastor she is now able to hear the Lord's Prayer as a prayer of assurance, not condemnation. Perhaps she can deal with the guilt dimensions of this episode—the wrong she did to the rival candidate—now that she has revealed her shameful self ("forgive us our sins, as we forgive those who sin against us"). On the other hand, the pastor's recourse to the Lord's Prayer (a rather unimaginative pastoral act) reveals much about him and his role as personal comforter, the issue to which we now direct our attention.

Ministering to Shame

We have said that the Christian response to pain is to seek to intensify our sense of exposure, for this is the way for us to overcome the isolating effects of our pain. Given her impending death and the fact that the episode was depriving her of peace of mind in her final days, Mrs. A was now motivated to expose herself, though not fully. She did not want to tell her story to her home pastor, and she was hesitant to provide the full details of the episode. What was the lie she told about the other woman? Would this begin to reveal the full depths of her shame? Thus a part of her wanted exposure and another part wanted to hide. Unfortunately, the pastor's response to her "confession" favored the hiding, and the side of her that sought exposure was visibly disappointed. "I hope I haven't bored you."

The reason his response to her story had this effect was not simply that he had failed to diagnose the problem as basically one of shame rather than guilt. The deeper problem was that he was not motivated by personal disposition or theological conviction to help her to expose herself even more. He had heard enough—enough to permit him to leave the episode itself behind and begin to express a few clichés about Christian life, faith, forgiveness, and the nature of God. And because the woman's self-exposure was terminated just as it was beginning to get somewhere her sense of isolation was not reduced, much less overcome. His recitation of the Lord's Prayer and her expressed hope that she had not bored him suggest that she felt just as isolated as before.

What could he have done differently? Basically, he could have encouraged her to reveal details of the story that she had not yet disclosed and together they could have probed the story for every possible meaning it might have had for her self-understanding. As this exploration proceeded, the two of them would undoubtedly have recognized that she was exposing herself—her shameful self—not only to the pastor but also to God. God's own perspective on her self-disclosure would then become clear to her. Perhaps this would result in the perception that God views her shameful deed with eyes of forgiveness, leading her to say not "I suppose forgiveness is ours" but "I know forgiveness is mine." But there could also be more: the perception of God's love reaching out to her, lifting her up, and calling her by name. Then would the isolating effects of her pain be transcended, and her distinctiveness as God's child confirmed. As the love of God thus lifted her spirits, the pastor would know that he had helped to comfort her and make her feel more "at home" in the world and more "at peace" with herself in her last days on earth. For the ultimate comfort is not release from pain, but the conviction that nothing can separate us from the love of God.

In chapter 5 I will discuss the "personal comforter" role of the pastor in light of the wisdom tradition of ancient Israel. Like the pastoral roles of moral counselor and ritual coordinator, this role is also emphasized by the wisdom tradition, especially through its portrayal of Job's counselors.

CHAPTER 5

Pastoral Care
as
Therapeutic Wisdom

A striking feature of Erikson's schedule of virtues and of his stages of ritualization is that both culminate in wisdom. The virtue of the eighth stage is wisdom, and in the eighth stage of the ritualization process the mature adult is viewed as the personification of ritual wisdom. That both moral development and the ritualization process culminate in wisdom is good reason for us to explore the possible affinities between Erikson's life cycle theory and the wisdom tradition of ancient Israel.

ERIKSON'S AFFINITIES WITH
THE WISDOM TRADITION

In this chapter I hope to establish the basic fact that Erikson's life cycle theory fits well with the wisdom tradition. I do not mean to suggest that his theory reflects any direct influence from the wisdom tradition but only that the two exhibit a similar orientation to life, even in specific details. In demonstrating this affinity I will be providing biblical grounding for the pastoral care model proposed in this book, a model based on the pastoral roles of moral counselor, ritual coordinator, and personal comforter. I will call this model "therapeutic wisdom."

Three books comprise the bulk of the biblical wisdom tradition—Proverbs, Ecclesiastes, and Job. A useful way to understand what these three books have in common, and yet what also distinguishes each, is to pick up on the orientation theme to which I have repeatedly alluded. As noted in the conclusion to chapter 1 there are three major types of disorienting experiences: moral confusion, inability to comprehend life's meaning and purpose, and severe suffering. The three wisdom books address these issues. The Book of Proverbs is concerned with moral clarity, Ecclesiastes with life's meaning and purpose, and Job with extreme suffering.

As we have seen, Erikson's life cycle theory is concerned with all three issues, though his perspective on life comes closest to that of Proverbs. So my comments on the affinities between Erikson's life cycle theory and the wisdom tradition will focus mainly on Proverbs. In exploring these affinities I will follow the general outline of the present book, beginning with the similarities between Erikson's basic life cycle theory and Proverbs' world view, then moving to more specific affinities in their approach to moral concerns, ritual, and the problem of personal suffering. I will conclude the chapter by discussing the three pastoral roles—moral counselor, ritual coordinator, and personal comforter—from the wisdom tradition perspective.

Proverbs and Erikson's Basic Theory

The basic scientific concept in Erikson's life cycle theory is the epigenetic principle, to which we referred in chapter 1. This concept holds that "anything that grows has a ground plan, and that out of this ground plan the parts arise, each part having its time of special ascendency, until all parts have arisen to form a functioning whole."[1] This means that growth follows a certain preestablished order which is reflected in an orderly time sequence and in the interconnections between the various parts that make up the whole. All growing things have an epigenetic ground plan, and this means that there is order in all creation.

Order in the World

Among the three wisdom books Proverbs is the most confident that such order is there if we can only discern it. Gerhard von Rad identifies two strategies that Proverbs employs for dealing more effectively with the world: the observation of order and cause-and-effect reasoning. He also shows that both strategies are designed to identify the order that exists in the world of experience.[2]

With respect to the first of these two strategies—observation of order—the writers of Proverbs discern order in the natural world, the social world (the world of human interaction), and the psychological world (the "inner life"). Their conclusion that such order exists is based on many different kinds of observation. One involves observing the temporal order in the natural and social world; the writers see that for everything there is a time and season, and that attempts to change this order through haste inevitably fail. Another is based on the observation that even situations which seem to challenge our confidence in such order (puzzling events in nature, curious behavior in society, or contradictory emotions in the inner life) actually confirm that such order exists, because these anomalies are repeated over and over again and become predictable.

A third kind of observation of order involves noting the similarities between two or more spheres (natural, social, or psychological). Many proverbs draw analogies between two spheres, thus establishing a connection between two orders of life. A favorite method of the proverbs is to use the natural world to shed light on the social world or on the psychological world: "Like clouds and wind without rain is a man who boasts of a gift he does not give" (Prov. 25:14). "As in water face answers to face, so the mind of man reflects the man" (27:19). Linkage of the social world to the inner world is also common: "A man without self-control is like a city broken into and left without walls" (25:28). By drawing such analogies between the various spheres Proverbs makes a modest but genuine step toward the notion that there is an all-embracing order to life. As von Rad points out: "One could almost say that the further apart the subjects being compared lay, the more interesting must the discovery of analogies have been, insofar as this revealed something of the breadth of the order that was discovered."[3]

The second strategy for demonstrating order in the world involves cause-and-effect reasoning. The previous strategy linked two or more dimensions of life, placing them side by side and noting their similarities. This one discerns a natural succession of events. In its cause-and-effect reasoning Proverbs gives primacy to moral order. Many proverbs make the point that an evil deed has disastrous consequences while good deeds result in blessing: "Pride goes before destruction, and a haughty spirit before a fall" (Prov. 16:18). "A soft answer turns away wrath, but a harsh word stirs up anger" (15:1). Von Rad says that such proverbs are not stating a doctrine of divine retribution but affirming the existence of a moral order: "These sentences are not concerned with a divine, juridical act which subsequently deals out to men blessing or punishment, but with an order of life which can be experienced."[4] The Book of Proverbs recognizes that there is much skepticism about the claim that good is rewarded and bad is punished. (Ecclesiastes and Job also raise serious questions about this very claim.) It bases its confidence in moral order on the grounds that good and evil are self-fulfilling. They accomplish what they set out to accomplish: evil produces evil, good effects good. The confidence that evil is punished and good results in blessing is not merely a naive optimism about the moral order. Proverbs is basically confident about the world and its essential order, but it bases this optimism on observation of how good actions are "life-promoting forces" which effect what they set out to effect.

To Proverbs this discernment of order in the world and in human experience is important because it provides a fundamental orientation to life. To be able to discern life's order and to take action on the basis of this perceived order is to have a basic orientation to life. A person so oriented makes connections between the various spheres of life and uses knowledge gained in one sphere to understand another. A person oriented in this way is also able to live in the present with an eye toward the future, putting good into effect today in order to reap its benefits tomorrow.

Proverbs and Erikson share a common belief in the world order and base it on similar factors. Both emphasize the temporal order, in which what is done in the present has consequences far into the future. Thus Erikson emphasizes the mother's role in evoking the infant's pervasive attitude of trust, and Proverbs advises parents to "train up a child in the way he should go, and when he is old he will not depart from it" (Prov. 22:6). Also, both stress the interconnections between the various spheres of life, particularly similarities between the natural world and the world of human experience. Here Erikson's comparisons of human ritualization to that of animals is especially relevant, for example, the greeting ritual between mother geese and their new offspring (which he compares to the greeting ritual between the human mother and her child),[5] and the antler tournament among the Damstags (which he compares with Gandhi's method of militant nonviolence).[6] We might also note Erikson's emphasis on Luther's use of the sow as a metaphor of the spiritual life,[7] and Erikson's criticism of politicized youths' "use of the appelation 'pigs,' which certainly showed a strange lack of respect for an innocently muddy animal."[8]

Developmental Approach to Life

But Erikson's life cycle theory is developmental, and much of its claim that life has a fundamental order is based on his developmental perspective with its epigenetic principle and emphasis on the succession of generations. Does the wisdom tradition have anything like a developmental approach to life? Biblical scholars say that it does. Many question von Rad's view that the story of Joseph's development from a young Jew in exile to a powerful Egyptian leader belongs in the wisdom tradition.[9] But they agree that the wisdom tradition took a developmental approach to life, emphasizing the development of moral character. This is especially evident in the role assigned child-rearing in the development of mature moral character; and the emphasis given, especially in Proverbs, to the fact that good children are a credit to their parents and vice versa: "He who begets a wise son will be glad in him" (Prov. 23:24) and "The glory of sons is their fathers" (17:6). This developmental approach is also evident in Proverbs' many warnings that a young man must find a good marriage partner or suffer for the rest of his days. But it is perhaps most evident in Proverbs' use of the metaphor of the journey of life. As James Crenshaw points out: "The notion of a path was particularly appropriate in the thinking of Israel's wise men and women, for at birth everyone had embarked on a journey which led to a full life or to premature departure." The wise ones recognized that God could overrule human itineraries: "Nevertheless, the wise journeyed toward their ultimate destination with sure confidence that they would reach that place safely, whereas fools would lose their way."[10] This metaphor of the life journey, or traveling down the path of life, indicates that Proverbs has a developmental emphasis: "Let your eyes look directly forward, and your gaze be straight before you. Take heed to the path of your feet, then all your ways will be sure" (Prov. 4:25–26). (Other proverbs that reflect this developmental emphasis are to be found at Prov. 15:14; 16:17; and 24:30–34).

Proverbs also shares Erikson's emphasis on the social matrix within which an individual grows and matures. Like Erikson with his widening social radius and ritualized encounters, Proverbs emphasizes that development is not an individual achievement but a societal task. As Crenshaw points out, Israel's teachers

> developed the notion of wisdom as a guard who watched over the sages while they slept. With this idea they arrived remarkably close to the modern concept of culture or "ethos," that powerful network of sanctions that all individuals unconsciously assimilate just as naturally as they eat and breathe.[11]

This understanding of development squares well with Erikson's own view of development as a complex interplay between an ever-widening radius of social interaction and the cogwheeling of generations.

I would also draw attention to Erikson's use of a bipolar structure involving a positive and negative pole in each stage to conceptualize the developmental process. In an article entitled "Wisdom and Pastoral Theology" Walter Harrelson notes how Proverbs works with polar opposites: good and evil, hot and cold, life and death, wisdom and folly. He says that "all these are the stock in trade of the wisdom school" and claims that "the structure of human thought depends upon such polar opposites," that "such contrasts . . . help to shape man's experience and provide orientation toward his world."[12] Erikson's use of polar opposites in his psychosocial stages is clearly relevant here. Especially significant is his insistence that the negative pole is as vital as the positive pole for one's orientation in the world. As the wisdom tradition recognized, it is not the positive pole alone but the contrast between positive and negative that provides an orientation to one's world.

Other affinities between Erikson's theory and the wisdom tradition could be cited, and those mentioned here could be greatly expanded, but enough has been said to make the point that on theoretical grounds alone Erikson and the wisdom tradition have much in common.

Proverbs and Erikson's Moral Emphases

I have already noted how both Erikson and Proverbs take special interest in moral order, and how they both view such order in developmental terms. But other important connections between Erikson and the wisdom tradition can be noted here.

First, there is the fact that Erikson takes considerable interest in moral and ethical issues yet does not attempt to develop his views into a comprehensive ethical system or model. He is similar to the wisdom tradition in this regard. Walter Harrelson points out that in Proverbs "wisdom operates without the necessity of synthesis." It is not a systematic philosophy or ethical system but a large collection of "observation that can be applied to given situations unthinkingly, immediately, without necessary reference to some coherent scheme of thought with which they fit."[13] Like Proverbs, Erikson prefers to make astute moral observation about human experience rather than formulate ethical theory. When invited by Richard Evans to add a final word to their dialogue on Erikson's work, Erikson told a story:

> You have heard of the rabbi who felt inhibited when he was asked to make a speech in heaven. "I am good only at refutation," he said. My difficulty is different. I find it hard to put up a good argument, because I am more at home in observation and illustration.[14]

Being more at home in observation and illustration than in argument places Erikson in the "wisdom" approach to moral issues.

Second, the fact that Erikson views wisdom as the highest virtue of the moral life means that he differs from ethicists who give primacy to *justice*. One reason why attempts to reconcile Erikson's life cycle theory and Lawrence Kohlberg's theory of moral development have not been successful is that Erikson stresses wisdom while Kohlberg emphasizes justice.[15] In biblical terms this places Kohlberg more squarely in the prophetic tradition. Erikson's differences with moral theories oriented to justice are partly due to his view that moral conflict begins with the "autonomy vs. shame and doubt" stage, not the "initiative vs. guilt" stage.[16] This may also explain Erikson's affinities with the moral perspective of Proverbs which is clearly more concerned with shame issues than with guilt issues. Various proverbs speak directly of "being put to shame" and others address shameful experiences (such as being publicly humiliated, suffering disgrace, acting like a fool, bringing shame on one's relatives, suffering rebuke, appearing lazy, and maintaining one's "good name").

Third, and most important, there are clear affinities between Erikson and the wisdom tradition on the matter of virtues and vices. In my *Biblical Approaches to Pastoral Counseling* I noted that Erikson's schedule of virtues has direct parallels in the Book of Proverbs; I listed verses on hope, will, purpose, competence, fidelity, love, care, and wisdom.[17] The same can be done in the case of my schedule of vices. Here are some selected examples:

1. Gluttony: "Be not among winebibbers, or among gluttonous eaters of meat; for the drunkard and the glutton will come to poverty, and drowsiness will clothe a man with rags" (23:20–21).

2. Anger: "A soft answer turns away wrath, but a harsh word stirs up anger" (15:1). "He who is slow to anger has great understanding, but he who has a hasty temper exalts folly" (14:29).

3. Greed: "All day long the wicked covets, but the righteous gives and does not hold back" (21:26).

4. Envy: "Let not your heart envy sinners, but continue in the fear of the Lord all day" (23:17).

5. Pride: "Pride goes before destruction, and a haughty spirit before a fall. It is better to be of a lowly spirit with the poor than to divide the spoil with the proud" (16:18–19).

6. Lust: "Can a man carry fire in his bosom and his clothes not be burned?" (6:27). "He who commits adultery has no sense; he who does it destroys himself" (6:32).

7. Indifference: "A little sleep, a little slumber, a little folding of the hands to rest, and poverty will come upon you like a robber, and want like an armed man" (24:33–34).

8. Melancholy: "A glad heart makes a cheerful countenance, but by sorrow of heart the spirit is broken" (15:13).

These proverbs suggest that avoiding the deadly vices is not motivated by a negative, life-rejecting, moralistic orientation to the world. Rather, the avoidance of vice is life-affirming. As Crenshaw puts it, the wise engage in conduct that "secures existence."[18] Thus Prov. 4:23: "Keep your heart with all vigilance; for from it flow the springs of life." In contrast, the vices grow out of a basic antipathy to real engagement in life. It is not the wise but the foolish who reflect Erikson's basic antipathies of withdrawal, compulsion, inhibition, inertia, repudiation, exclusivity, rejectivity, and disdain.[19]

Proverbs and Erikson's Ritual Theory

The affinities between Erikson's theory of ritualization and the wisdom tradition are fundamental in character. The priestly group in ancient Israel was concerned with the society's special rituals and rites, while the wisdom group was concerned with the ritualization of everyday life. One reason the wisdom teachers of ancient Israel are difficult to locate sociologically is that they were involved in the everyday life of the community, not in special orders. It seems appropriate to call them teachers but not in the sense that they were an intellectual elite. As Crenshaw points out, the proverbial tradition undoubtedly began in the families or clans then spread gradually to the political arena, where wisdom teachers may have been counselors to kings. It was not until the intertestamental period that the wisdom tradition developed schools in which there was a formal teacher-student relationship.[20] Given its roots in the family the wisdom tradition was concerned with the ritualization of everyday life. In fact, this ritualization process is essentially what the proverbs are all about.

Some proverbs describe the everyday ritual of business transactions: "'It is bad, it is bad,' says the buyer; but when he goes away, then he boasts" (Prov. 20:14). Other proverbs concern the ritualization of everyday neighborliness: "He who blesses his neighbor with a loud voice, rising early in the morning, will be counted as cursing" (27:14). Others concern the ritualization of interpersonal communications: "A rebuke goes deeper into a man of understanding than a hundred blows into a fool" (17:10). Some deal with the ritualization of family interaction: "Better is a dry morsel with quiet than a houseful of feasting with strife" (17:1); "Discipline your son while there is hope; do not set your heart on his destruction" (19:18). Or courtship: "Three things are too wonderful for me; four I do not understand: the way of an eagle in the sky, the way of a serpent on a rock, the way of a ship on the high seas, and the way of a man with a maiden" (30:18–19). Or daily work: "He who is slack in his work is a brother to him who destroys" (18:9). These few examples show that Proverbs is deeply concerned with the ritualization of everyday life. Few aspects of this ritualization process escape its purview.

Moreover, Proverbs believes that wise ritualization will support the moral order so that everyday rituals and the moral order go hand in hand.

Erikson shares the wisdom tradition's desire to emphasize the ritualization of everyday life and to leave the more specific rites and ceremonies to others. As we have seen, this is obviously true of his writings on the ritual process. This is also evident in his recent essay on the Galilean sayings of Jesus where he observes that the official rituals of the Jewish community in Jesus' time had lost their capacity to renew and rejuvenate the nation. This was possibly because they had become "dominated by a compulsive scrupulosity."[21] But Erikson notes that "there was, and is, in the Jewish community a ritualization of everyday life which must have played a great role in the survival of Judaism. I am referring to family life."[22] In discussing Jesus' own career Erikson cites numerous instances in which Jesus made everyday ritualization an essential part of his work and vision. Jesus did this through his joyous table fellowship with tax collectors and sinners, through his transformation of prayer into an intimate conversation with his Father, through his use of close physical contact as a means of healing, and through the ritual of story-telling. Erikson believes that Jesus, in giving everyday ritualization central importance, provided a new and more inclusive sense of "We" through a new conception of the kingdom of God as "shared companionship."[23]

Do Erikson and the wisdom tradition have similar conceptions of the ritualization process? Do they emphasize the same ritual elements? Erikson's ritual elements seem appropriate for describing how Proverbs orders its life. Many proverbs reflect the judicious element (emphasizing the importance of sound child-rearing procedures), the dramatic element (with the ideal role of the wise posed against the negative role of the foolish), the formal (with emphasis on performing disciplined work), the ideological (emphasizing that the wise allow God to direct their paths), the affiliative (maintaining sound, noncontentious relationships with friends, neighbors, and family members), the generational (parents deeply involved in their children's moral formation), and the integral (with emphasis on the personal integrity of those who live wisely).

The numinous element is also reflected in Proverbs, though it presents special difficulties in interpretation. There are proverbs that personify wisdom as a woman, and their emotional tone suggests that she mediates the numinous to those who desire her. Moreover, there is some indication that these proverbs view the relationship between Wisdom and those who seek her in terms of mother-child dynamics. Wisdom is like a mother whose counsel is life-giving.[24] True, Proverbs has a tendency to emphasize the importance of parental discipline (stage 2) over maternal love (stage 1). Still, by personifying wisdom, the wisdom tradition recognized the role of the numinous in the ritualization of everyday life. And the wisdom tradition may have set the stage for Christianity's emphasis on the numinous element through its imagery of the Nativity.[25]

Proverbs and Erikson on Counseling

I have touched on the affinities between Proverbs and Erikson with respect to the question of shame in chapter 4. But chapter 4 was also concerned with the pastor's role as personal comforter, which raises the question of the affinities between Erikson and the wisdom tradition on the issue of personal counseling.

Erikson's only sustained discussion of counseling appears in his essay, "The Nature of Clinical Evidence,"[26] and he does not make any systematic effort in this essay to link his views on counseling to his life cycle theory. However, he offers a detailed discussion of one of his own counseling cases (involving a young seminarian who had interrupted his studies to enter psychiatric treatment), and this case is directly relevant to the wisdom tradition's approach to counseling. I will not attempt to summarize the case here nor to note the many parallels between his interpretation of this case and wisdom tradition concerns. But this is especially noteworthy: Erikson says he felt he was being challenged by the young man "to prove, all at once, the goodness of mothers, the immortality of grandfathers, my own perfection, and God's grace."[27] This same complaint could have been voiced by Job's counselors. And they too, like Erikson, could have informed their suffering neighbor that they were only trying to help him "understand what was behind his helplessness."[28]

There is general agreement among biblical scholars that the men who counseled Job (Eliphaz, Bildad, and Zophar) reflect the wisdom tradition as represented in Proverbs. But there is much disagreement among scholars concerning the genre of the Book of Job, whether it is a debate (disputation) or a lament.[29] Those who take the former position tend to see Job's friends as moral counselors who are trying to help him restore his life through an effective plan for the future. Those who take the latter view see Job's companions as personal comforters, standing by their friend in his pain and suffering. When they are viewed as moral counselors, their role is perceived as quasi-official, as though they are under obligation to persuade Job to acknowledge his wrongdoing.[30] When they are viewed as personal comforters, their role seems much less official and far more voluntary, an expression of good will no matter how ineffective their efforts proved to be.

The truth of the matter may be that Job's friends perceive themselves as moral counselors dealing with what they see as Job's moral confusion, while Job perceives himself as lamenting, pressed to the limits of his capacity to endure suffering. This would explain why, as Crenshaw puts it, "Job and friends talk past one another."[31] This also explains why Job's counselors seem strident and insensitive, as when Eliphaz in obvious frustration asks Job, "Are the consolations of God too small for you?" (Job 15:11). Most important, this fundamental difference in their approach to Job's disorienting experience (moral confusion vs. extreme suffering) led them to quite different interpretations of what was behind his helplessness. Job's counselors reaffirmed their belief in the essential order of life and encouraged him to repent of any wrongdoing so that the process of moral recovery could begin. But Job viewed his situation as one of unaccountable suffering and sought answers to the question of why he was having to suffer for no good reason. Crenshaw suggests that the answer Job received through his audience with God was that God may act in absolute freedom:

> God taught his servant the error in assuming that the universe operated according to a principle of rationality. Once that putative principle of order collapsed before divine freedom, the need for personal vindication vanished as well, since God's anger and favor show no positive correspondence with human acts of villainy or virtue. Job's personal experience had taught him that last bit of information, but he had also clung tenaciously to an assumption of order. Faced with a stark reminder of divine freedom, Job finally gave up this comforting claim, which had hardly brought solace in his case.[32]

This distinction between order and freedom suggests that the pastor's roles as moral counselor and personal comforter need to center on different features of God's being in the world. As moral counselors, Job's friends stressed God's maintenance of order in the world. But had they perceived their role as that of personal comforters they would have wanted to stress the freedom of God. That God acts freely was much more comforting to Job than that God maintains order. For if inflicting pain on Job was a free act of God, then God was also free to release Job from his suffering. For those who are suffering, God's freedom to act without any constraints whatsoever can be the source of consolation. The prayers of David as his son was dying and of Jesus in the garden of Gethsemane are vivid examples of suffering men who prayed with absolute freedom because they were conscious that God could also respond with absolute freedom.[33] In short, it makes a difference whether we perceive ourselves to be doing moral counseling or personal comforting. In the one we will stress God's order. In the other we will emphasize God's freedom. The case of Job and his counselors illustrates the importance of avoiding "genre" errors in pastoral work with disoriented individuals.

WISDOM AND PASTORAL IMAGES

Having explored the affinities between Erikson and the wisdom tradition I now want to formulate a pastoral model based on these affinities. To lay the groundwork for this we need to take a brief look at another pastoral image that has emerged in recent years, directing our attention toward the wisdom tradition. This is the model of pastoral care based on the image of the pastor as a clown or a fool. In its original formulation this model had little to do with the concerns of the wisdom tradition. In fact, it seems directly antithetical to the wisdom tradition, which is critical of fools—does not abide fools cheerfully, or suffer them gladly! More recently, however, this pastoral image has been taking on new dimensions that bring it closer to the perspectives of the wisdom tradition.

The Clown

As originally put forward by Heije Faber, this image of the pastor as clown took note of the similarities between the clown in the circus and the minister in the hospital.[34] Faber pointed out that the clown is one of the circus acts but is also unique, set apart from the other acts. The clown appears like an amateur among highly skilled professionals, yet the clown's achievement of creative spontaneity is the result of considerable training. Thus the clown seems an apt image for the chaplain who may appear like an amateur among professionals but is required to respond to many difficult situations with a professional's spontaneity.

More recently, David Switzer has picked up on Faber's image of the clown and has suggested that the following characteristics of the clown are also characteristic of the pastor in the hospital setting:[35]

1. The clown is the genuinely human thread that runs through the entire circus, holding it together as a coherent and meaningful process.

2. The clown represents humanity, and serves as a point of contact with the audience (patient and family), sharing the same gamut of emotion. Unlike the "expert technicians" (medical staff), the clown is close to the audience and reflects their feelings as they and the clown observe the work of the other performers.

3. The clown is highly trained, a competent professional whose professional acts grow out of a deep identification with humanity.

4. The clown's real identity is disguised by the mask, but clowns' effectiveness is never separated from their being as persons. Erikson calls this "disciplined subjectivity."[36]

The Wise Fool

In *Rediscovering Pastoral Care* Alastair Campbell takes up the clown image once again.[37] He has modified the image, however, calling it "wise folly." This shifts the image from the circus clown to "the disheveled, gauche, tragicomic figure of the fool."[38]

In this shift Campbell is not as concerned as Faber or Switzer to affirm that this figure is highly professional. The professional function and role of Campbell's wise fool are deliberately more ambiguous than those of Faber's clown. This is evident in Campbell's list of the characteristics of the wise fool: (1) simplicity (Campbell has in mind the simpleton who with disarming naiveté exposes insincerity and self-deception); (2) loyalty (a foolhardy disregard of self out of a higher loyalty to God); and (3) prophecy (disclosing the bankruptcy of established ways of doing things by engaging in incongruous acts that reflect a deeper humanity). If we took the fool more seriously in pastoral care Campbell believes there would be greater use of simple language and simple ways of relating to one another, greater attention to the value of loyal commitment which would not be so limited by the professional setting and roles, and greater evidence of the joyousness of faith which announces and enacts a more "graceful" attitude toward life.

By viewing this model as "wise" folly Campbell suggests that pastoral care needs to be founded more on simple wisdom. The folly he advocates is certainly not the stupidity that the wisdom teachers designate folly. It is the *wise* folly extolled in 1 Cor. 3:18: "If anyone among you thinks he is wise by this world's standards, he should become a fool, in order to be really wise" (author paraphrase). Thus Campbell opens the possibility of a pastoral model based on wisdom by drawing attention to the interplay between wisdom and folly.

THERAPEUTIC WISDOM

Building on these precursors, but drawing more self-consciously on the wisdom tradition, I propose a pastoral model called "therapeutic wisdom"—the term Erikson uses to describe the role Staupitz played in the life of the young Luther.[39] While the model needs fuller elaboration than I can give it here the basic idea behind the model is to place the pastoral roles we have been discussing into the context of the wisdom tradition, thus giving these roles (individually and collectively) a biblical rootage. Let us look at the three pastoral roles in terms of the wisdom tradition.

The Moral Counselor

Walter Harrelson and Walter Brueggemann, both biblical scholars, have applied the wisdom tradition's understanding of the role of moral counselor to contemporary ministry. Harrelson suggests that the wisdom tradition offers a unique alternative to the two major approaches to moral issues in ethical thinking today. It neither attempts to "define the good for man in some total and all-inclusive system" (philosophical ethics) nor does it "assume that the situation itself must shape and dictate decisions" (situational ethics).[40] Rather,

> the wisdom tradition would give us examples of various kinds of con-
> duct and let us learn what we can from such examples. It would give
> these to us in sharp pictures, deeply etched into the consciousness,
> taught to us when young, not sprung on us only as needed.[41]

Harrelson notes that this use of illustrative examples to structure our thinking about moral issues is the method employed by advice columnists in daily newspapers. These columnists have become the wisdom teachers of today, providing moral counsel through the publication of letters dealing with moral problems of widespread interest.

While pastors may resist comparison with advice columnists, their methods of moral counsel have significant similarities. The moral counsel provided by pastors involves educating and advising their parishioners through stories and images, not abstract philosophical principles. This may include moral persuasion through sermon illustrations, sharing personal family anecdotes during premarital counseling, discussing the lives of exemplary Christians in confirmation classes, using graphic imagery to make a moral point in children's sermons, or interpreting issues in medical ethics in light of pastoral experiences with ailing and dying parishioners. Pastoral theology demonstrates the value of this approach to moral issues through its use of verbatim material, and religious educators employ this approach through their instructional use of stories involving difficult moral dilemmas. The use of such methods is quite compatible with the wisdom tradition's approach to moral counsel. Such methods ensure that moral concerns will be addressed in their contextual setting. At the same time there is the implicit if not explicit expectation that use of these stories will enable pastors and parishioners to formulate a more general set of convictions regarding moral conduct and the formation of moral character.

In comparing the wisdom teacher with the king, priest, and prophets of ancient Israel, Walter Brueggemann says that wisdom teachers served as counselors to kings and persons in high authority.

Their function was to provide these leaders with a perspective on the problems confronting the nation. In general this meant a perspective informed by moral considerations which the leader, under political pressures, might otherwise overlook. Thus for Brueggemann the primary role of the wisdom teacher was to engage in moral counsel relating to difficult political, social and institutional problems.[42]

Brueggemann has a similar view of the contemporary pastor's role as moral counselor. Many parishioners are in positions of responsibility in their professional and community life. Such persons often need a "reflective presence to discern hidden issues, to ask about obscure opportunities, to think through options and resources, and to ask about the relation between private and communal good."[43] To address this need pastors are encouraged to follow the procedure of the wisdom teachers which means putting the question of meaning with discernment, making their observations out of real experiences, and enlarging the vision from which people make their decisions. Above all pastors' moral counselor roles are more informal than the pastoral roles of priest and prophet which means that their legitimacy as moral counselors derives less from their official status and more from their capacity to be inherently helpful.[44]

The Ritual Coordinator

Because they identify ritual with the priestly class, biblical scholars do not help us much toward understanding how the wisdom tradition may inform the pastoral role of ritual coordinator. But our preceding discussion of Proverbs' perspective on ritual gives us valuable clues.

First, this discussion helps us to see that the pastor's wisdom or capacity for discernment is not a personal gift but a reflection of the ritual wisdom of the community. The wise remain anonymous in the wisdom tradition. No one except Solomon is singled out as having uncommon personal wisdom, and his reputation for being wise was due mainly to his great wealth. (The reasoning: anyone that wealthy must have been wise!)[45] Thus wisdom resides in the community, not the individual. On the other hand it is not unreasonable to expect that pastors together with laity will begin to personify the ritual wisdom of the community during the course of their life's journey. If the wisdom tradition does not identify persons who are uncommonly wise, it does say that wisdom is available to those who are willing to conform their lives to the ritual wisdom of the community.

Second, our previous discussion enables us to see that the pastor's major purpose as ritual coordinator is to help persons become better oriented in the world. The wisdom tradition did not turn to general philosophical or ethical principles but instead looked to its ritualization processes for such orientation. The orientation provided then, as now, is similar to the sacred pole in Eliade's tale. This means that it provided a point of reference, but it also means that this was not a fixed point. Given its developmental perspective on life—life viewed as a journey—the wisdom tradition did not insist on fixed points of reference. Only much later in the history of ancient Israel did the wisdom tradition attempt to provide such a fixed location by merging wisdom and the law.[46] However, because it relinquished such fixed points of reference, it became all the more crucial that it be able to point to regularities and predictable patterns in life. Otherwise there would be no basis of orientation at all. It was the task of the ritual wisdom of the community to identify such regularities and thereby provide a sense of order which served to keep persons oriented in a changing world.

Erikson is a valuable contemporary resource here because he is struggling with the same issues. He too takes a developmental perspective on human life and thus accepts the absence of fixed reference points. But this also makes him all the more concerned to find regularities and predictable patterns in the developmental process itself. In a recent discussion of this very issue he points out that Albert Einstein's theory of relativity did away with absolute, fixed points, but it replaced them with regularities between two moving entities (like the relation of two moving railroad trains to one another). As Erikson puts it, relativity "at first had unbearably relativistic implications, seemingly undermining the foundations of any firm human 'standpoint'; and yet, it opens a new vista in which relative standpoints are 'reconciled' to each other in fundamental invariance."[47] He also points out that our sense of being oriented in the world does not require rootedness in a geographical location, but it does mean being able to understand ourselves as participants in a meaningful cogwheeling of generations. (The respective generations are relative standpoints which are reconciled to one another in fundamental invariance.) Thus for Erikson as for the wisdom tradition, there is no fixed point of reference but at best a patterned regularity.[48]

Erikson also recognizes that his own life cycle theory may serve a ritual function by providing reference points as we journey through life. If we know what stages await us, and what kinds of psychosocial conflicts we can expect at each stage, this helps us maintain our sense of orientation in the world. Mindful that his theory may be used in this fashion Erikson expresses the hope that it will not be used to structure lives in a ritualistic fashion and thus "take the game out of growing up."[49] This is undoubtedly a danger. But most interpreters of the contemporary scene note that we seem almost desperate for ways to give pattern to our lives. Robert Jay Lifton says that life for moderns is increasingly protean, or formless, lacking any real sense of continuity and order.[50] In light of this assessment we should not be overly worried that Erikson's life cycle theory might be used to ritual excess.

In short, the challenge the pastor faces as ritual coordinator is to help persons experience order in their lives while recognizing that there are no fixed points. But where does the pastor turn for convincing expressions of order? Note that we call it the wisdom *tradition.* In their concern for temporal as opposed to spatial orientation, the wisdom teachers themselves did not seek order in temples and sacred places but in what Erikson calls "living tradition"—the "orders and objects and sayings" that link us to men and women of distant times and pursuits.[51] This does not mean of course that the pastor must turn to the wisdom tradition itself. This is only one of many traditions. But one important feature of the wisdom tradition that makes it especially relevant to our context of relativity is the fact that the three canonical wisdom books (Proverbs, Ecclesiastes, Job) do not reflect a single fixed point from which to orient ourselves. Instead, they are three relative standpoints which relate to one another in a certain fundamental invariance. Thus they comprise a tradition that fits our need for order-within-relativity.

The Personal Comforter

The personal comforter—this pastoral role addresses situations and crises that occur when the ritual process breaks down: when order becomes disorder. Many of the situations pastors face in their personal-comforter role involve breakdowns in the cogwheeling of generations. (Probably the most shattering experience in the whole series of sufferings visited on Job was the loss of his children.) Lifton points out that our confidence in the cogwheeling of generations has been severely undermined by the threat of nuclear holocaust.[52] Other less-global but certainly painful threats to our sense of the cogwheeling of generations are divorce (including battles over child custody), loss of ethnic and racial identity through intermarriage, inability to bear children, and various forms of premature death.

Proverbs is not oblivious to situations in which our confidence in the essential order of life is threatened. Many proverbs concern pain and sorrow: "The heart knows its own bitterness, and no stranger shares its joy" (Prov. 14:10). And there are proverbs that counsel compassion and sensitivity to the pain of others: "He who sings songs to a heavy heart is like one who takes off a garment on a cold day" (25:20). But pastors who turn to the wisdom tradition for insights into their role as personal comforters will probably rely more heavily on Job and Ecclesiastes, for both books have greater relevance for those who have lost the sense of continuity in their lives and are suffering because of it.

To help focus this appropriation of Job and Ecclesiastes two developmental theorists in the Eriksonian tradition should prove most helpful. Lifton has addressed themes central to the Book of Job, especially issues of death and survivorship,[53] while Daniel J. Levinson's work on middle adulthood is most relevant to the concerns of Ecclesiastes, which poses questions concerning life's meaning that are similar to Levinson's mid-life polarities—young vs. old, destruction vs. creation, and attachment vs. separateness.[54] (While the Preacher has traditionally been viewed as an old man, the problems he addresses are essentially mid-life problems, especially the gulf that exists between the younger generation and himself.) And of course Erikson is also relevant to Ecclesiastes, for the Preacher clearly has conflicts regarding generativity vs. stagnation, and the vice of indifference threatens to triumph over the virtue of care.

In short, the wisdom tradition focuses especially on forms of suffering that are caused by breakdowns in the orderly functioning of the life cycle. And there are few instances of severe pain that are not directly or indirectly related to such life cycle breakdowns.

Jesus as Wisdom Teacher

While based on the wisdom tradition reflected in Proverbs, Job, and Ecclesiastes, a pastoral model of "therapeutic wisdom" might also draw on the Gospels. This is because the teachings of Jesus belong in the wisdom tradition. Norman Perrin says that "the parable is a literary form developed in the wisdom movement,"[55] and Amos Wilder observes that "the parables of Jesus came out of the wisdom tradition of Israel."[56] The proverbial sayings of Jesus ("Leave the dead to bury the dead") also fit within the wisdom tradition; they are structurally similar to the aphoristic sayings in Proverbs. Thus the wisdom tradition survives in the parables and proverbial sayings of Jesus, and Wilder goes so far as to suggest that through these stories and sayings Jesus fused the "proverbial wisdom" attributed to Solomon and the "apocalyptic wisdom" attributed to Enoch: "He united both styles and brought both into direct relation with the realities of his time."[57]

What would be the effect of viewing the pastoral roles of moral counselor, ritual coordinator, and personal comforter against the background of Jesus' special contribution to the wisdom tradition? Basically, it would locate these pastoral roles more clearly within an eschatological context. At the risk of oversimplification we can say that the wisdom tradition of ancient Israel had two basic tendencies. The first, reflected in Job and Ecclesiastes, was a tendency toward skepticism.[58] The second, reflected in the extracanonical book of Sirach, was a tendency toward eschatological hope. Jesus' parables reflect this eschatological thrust. Thus they are firmly within the wisdom tradition, although they challenge the moral vision of Proverbs on grounds quite distinct from either Job or Ecclesiastes.

In the parables the kingdom of God is perceived as an eschatological reversal of the present. As Perrin puts it, the parables proclaim the coming kingdom of God "in dramatic reversal, in the clash of worlds, in the sudden, unexpected transection of the everyday by the incursion of the divine."[59] Also, building on the work of Rudolf Bultmann and William A. Beardslee, Perrin points out that the intensely eschatological context of Jesus' teaching has these effects on his proverbial sayings: they intensify the normal proverbial insight by pressing it to its limits, and they jolt hearers out of the project of making a continuous whole of their existence and into the passing of a judgment on that existence. Thus these sayings challenge hearers to a "radical questioning" of the assumptions on which they have previously secured their existence.[60]

For the pastoral model of "therapeutic wisdom" the eschatological thrust of Jesus' teachings means that we cannot view orientation to the world as mere adjustment to the world as we find it. When Erikson credits Staupitz with exercising therapeutic wisdom toward Luther, he does not say that Staupitz helped Luther become better adjusted! This eschatological thrust also means that there are times when our efforts to help persons become better oriented in the world clash with God's incursions in the world. Indeed, there are occasions in our work as moral counselors, ritual coordinators, and personal comforters when our perceptions of how God is active in the world require us to jolt persons out of the project of making a continuous whole of their existence. But the fact that our pastoral work is always performed in the context of this potential "clash of worlds" underscores our profound need for therapeutic wisdom in our exercise of pastoral care. This does not mean being "wise in [our] own eyes" (Prov. 3:7) but opening ourselves to God, the source of therapeutic wisdom: "Making your ear attentive to wisdom and inclining your heart to understanding" (Prov. 2:2) and you will discover the "fountain of life" (Prov. 13:14) that brings "healing to your flesh and refreshment to your bones" (Prov. 3:8). So let us attend with our ears and receive with our hearts the stories and sayings of Jesus who among the men and women of distant times and different pursuits is the very personification of therapeutic wisdom: "I am the way, and the truth, and the life" (John 14:6).

Notes

PREFACE

1. Donald Capps, *Pastoral Care: A Thematic Approach* (Philadelphia: Westminster Press, 1979).
2. Don S. Browning, *The Moral Context of Pastoral Care* (Philadelphia: Westminster Press, 1976).
3. Donald Capps, *Biblical Approaches to Pastoral Counseling* (Philadelphia: Westminster Press, 1981).

CHAPTER 1

1. Erik H. Erikson, *Childhood and Society,* 2d rev. ed. (New York: W. W. Norton, 1963), chap. 7; *Young Man Luther* (New York: W. W. Norton, 1958); and *Identity and the Life Cycle* (New York: International Universities Press, 1959), chap. 2.
2. Erik H. Erikson, *Insight and Responsibility* (New York: W. W. Norton, 1964), chap. 4.
3. Erik H. Erikson, "The Ontogeny of Ritualization in Man," in *Psychoanalysis: A General Psychology,* ed. Rudolph M. Loewenstein et al. (New York: International Universities Press, 1966); *Toys and Reasons: Stages in the Ritualization of Experience* (New York: W. W. Norton, 1977).
4. Erikson, *Childhood and Society,* 269.
5. Erikson, *Identity and the Life Cycle,* 52.
6. Robert Coles, *Erik H. Erikson: The Growth of His Work* (Boston: Little, Brown & Co., 1970), 137.
7. Erik H. Erikson, "On the Generational Cycle: An Address," *International Journal of Psycho-Analysis* 61 (1980):213–23.
8. Ibid., 215.
9. Erikson, *Childhood and Society,* 17.
10. Erik H. Erikson, *Identity: Youth and Crisis* (New York: W. W. Norton, 1968), 92.
11. Erik H. Erikson, *The Life Cycle Completed* (New York: W. W. Norton, 1982), 34–35.
12. Among Erikson's descriptions of the eight stages, my own favorite is

"The Life Cycle: Epigenesis of Identity," in *Identity: Youth and Crisis*, chap. 3. A fine analysis of the stages is given in Evelyn Eaton Whitehead and James D. Whitehead, *Christian Life Patterns* (Garden City, N. Y.: Doubleday Image Books, 1982).

13. Erikson, *Identity: Youth and Crisis*, 220.

14. Ibid.

15. Erikson, *Childhood and Society*, 266.

16. Erikson, *Identity: Youth and Crisis*, 140.

17. Ibid., 139.

18. Ibid.

19. Clifford E. Geertz, "Religion as a Cultural System," in *The Interpretation of Cultures* (New York: Basic Books, 1973), 87–125.

CHAPTER 2

1. Erikson, *Insight and Responsibility*, chap. 4.

2. Erikson, "Ontogeny of Ritualization."

3. Erikson, *Insight and Responsibility*, chap. 4.

4. Ibid., 139.

5. Erikson, *Life Cycle Completed*, 33.

6. Seward Hiltner, *Theological Dynamics* (Nashville: Abingdon, 1972), 92–98.

7. Ibid., 94.

8. Ibid., 97.

9. Ibid., 98.

10. Brian W. Grant, *From Sin to Wholeness* (Philadelphia: Westminster Press, 1982).

11. Ibid., 15.

12. On this point, see Erikson's essay on the golden rule in *Insight and Responsibility*, especially 222–23.

13. Stanford M. Lyman, *The Seven Deadly Sins: Society and Evil* (New York: St. Martin's Press, 1978). This is the major source for my discussion of the deadly vices. See also Henry Fairlie, *The Seven Deadly Sins Today* (Notre Dame, Ind.: University of Notre Dame Press, 1979).

14. The psychosocial modalities are adapted from the life cycle chart in Erikson's *Identity and the Life Cycle*, 166.

15. Erikson, *Insight and Responsibility*, 118.

16. Ibid., 119.

17. Ibid., 122.

18. Ibid., 124.

19. Ibid., 146.

20. Ibid., 125.

21. Ibid., 129–30.

22. Erikson, *Identity: Youth and Crisis*, chap. 7. Also, Erik H. Erikson, *Life History and the Historical Moment* (New York: W. W. Norton, 1975), 225–47.

23. Erikson, *Young Man Luther*, 213–14. See also Erik H. Erikson, *Gandhi's Truth: On the Origins of Militant Nonviolence* (New York: W. W. Norton, 1969), 398.

24. Erikson, *Insight and Responsibility*, 131.

25. Ibid., 133.

26. Newman S. Cryer, Jr., and John M. Vayhinger, eds., *Casebook in Pastoral Counseling* (Nashville: Abingdon, 1962), 267–70. I discussed this case at some length in my *Pastoral Counseling and Preaching* (Philadelphia: Westminster Press, 1980), 82–87.

27. Walter H. Capps points out that American soldiers in Vietnam experienced the inversion of their expected moral order. See his *The Unfinished War* (Boston: Beacon Press, 1982), 99–101.

28. Edgar N. Jackson, *A Psychology for Preaching* (Great Neck, N.Y.: Channel Press, 1961), chap. 2.

29. Benjamin Franklin, *The Autobiography of Benjamin Franklin* (New York: Washington Square Press, 1966), 100–102.

CHAPTER 3

1. Erikson, "Ontogeny of Ritualization."

2. Erikson, *Toys and Reasons*.

3. Erikson, *Life Cycle Completed*.

4. William H. Willimon, *Worship as Pastoral Care* (Nashville: Abingdon, 1979).

5. See Coval B. MacDonald, "Methods of Study in Pastoral Theology," in *The New Shape of Pastoral Theology*, ed. William B. Oglesby, Jr. (Nashville: Abingdon, 1969), 164–76.

6. Sigmund Freud, "Obsessive Actions and Religious Practices," in *The Standard Edition of the Complete Psychological Works of Sigmund Freud*, ed. James Strachey (London: The Hogarth Press, 1959), 9:115–27.

7. Erikson, *Toys and Reasons*, 83.

8. Ibid., 82.

9. Ibid., 85.

10. Ibid.

11. Ibid., 89.

12. Ibid., 91.

13. Ibid.

14. Ibid., 97.

15. See Donald Capps, "Erikson's Theory of Ritual: The Case of the Excommunication of Ann Hibbens," *Journal for the Scientific Study of Religion* 18 (1979):337–49.

16. Erikson, *Toys and Reasons*, 97.

17. See my analysis of the Ridge Park Presbyterian Church case in *Pastoral Care: A Thematic Approach*, chap. 2.

18. Erikson, *Toys and Reasons*, 101.

19. Ibid., 102.

20. Erikson, *Life Cycle Completed*, 48.

21. Erikson, *Toys and Reasons*, 99–100.

22. Erikson, *Life Cycle Completed*, 77.

23. Paul W. Pruyser, *A Dynamic Psychology of Religion* (New York: Harper & Row, 1968), 189.

24. Peter L. Berger, *A Rumor of Angels* (Garden City, N. Y.: Doubleday Anchor Books, 1970), 58.

25. Erikson, *Young Man Luther*, 222.

26. Erikson, *Toys and Reasons*, 103.

27. Ibid., 105.

28. Ibid., 106.

29. Erikson, *Young Man Luther*, 220.

30. Richard K. Fenn, *Liturgies and Trials* (New York: The Pilgrim Press, 1982), 107–8.

31. Donald Capps, "The Psychology of Petitionary Prayer," *Theology Today* 39 (1982):130–41.

32. Erikson, *Identity: Youth and Crisis*, 216–21. Erikson returns to this theme in "The Galilean Sayings and the Sense of 'I'," *The Yale Review* 70 (1981):321–62.

33. Erikson, *Toys and Reasons*, 110.

34. See LeRoy Aden, "Faith and the Developmental Cycle," *Pastoral Psychology* 24 (1976):215–30, for a model relating Erikson's eight stages to stages in faith.

35. Erikson, *Toys and Reasons*, 110.

36. Erikson, *Insight and Responsibility*, 131.

37. Erikson, *Toys and Reasons*, 112.

38. Erikson, *Life Cycle Completed*, 64.

39. Erikson, *Toys and Reasons*, 112.

40. Erikson, *Life Cycle Completed*, 65.

41. Ibid.

42. Ibid.

43. Teilhard de Chardin, *The Phenomenon of Man* (New York: Harper & Row, 1959), 153–55.

44. Mircea Eliade, *The Sacred and the Profane*, trans. Willard R. Trask (New York: Harper & Row, 1961), 32–34.

CHAPTER 4

1. Helen Merrell Lynd, *On Shame and the Search for Identity* (New York: Harcourt, Brace, 1958), chap. 2.

2. Ibid., 32.

3. John Dominic Crossan, *In Parables* (New York: Harper & Row, 1973), 85.

4. Sigmund Freud, *Civilization and Its Discontents*, ed. and trans. James Strachey (New York: W. W. Norton, 1962), 12.

5. Lynd, *Shame*, 27.

6. Elie Wiesel, *Night*, trans. Stella Rodway (New York: Avon Books, 1969), 121.

7. Lynd, *Shame*, 56.

8. Paul W. Pruyser, "The Ambiguities of Religion and Pain Control," *Theology Today* 38 (1981):6.

9. David Bakan, *Disease, Pain, and Sacrifice* (Chicago: University of Chicago Press, 1968), 57–58.

10. Augustine, *The Confessions of St. Augustine*, trans. John K. Ryan (Garden City, N. Y.: Doubleday, 1960).

11. Paul W. Pruyser, "Psychological Examination: Augustine," *Journal for the Scientific Study of Religion* 5 (1965–66):284–89. Quotation from 288.

12. Augustine, *Confessions*, 98.

13. Ibid., 112.

14. Lynd, *Shame*, 40.

15. Augustine, *Confessions*, 229.

16. Erikson, *Young Man Luther*, 213.

17. See Donald Capps, "Psychology of Petitionary Prayer," 137.

18. Henri Nouwen, *The Wounded Healer* (Garden City, N. Y.: Doubleday, 1972), 94.

19. Cryer and Vayhinger, *Pastoral Counseling*, 60–62.

CHAPTER 5

1. Erikson, *Identity: Youth and Crisis*, 92.

2. Gerhard von Rad, *Wisdom in Israel*, trans. James D. Martin (London: SCM Press, 1972), 113–37.

3. Ibid., 120.

4. Ibid., 129.

5. See Erikson, "Ontogeny of Ritualization."

6. Erikson, *Gandhi's Truth*, 425–26.

7. Erikson, *Young Man Luther*, 32–33.

8. Erikson, *Life History and the Historical Moment*, 212.

9. Gerhard von Rad, "The Joseph Narrative and Ancient Wisdom," in *The Problem of the Hexateuch and Other Essays* (Edinburgh: Oliver & Boyd, 1966), 292–300. James L. Crenshaw is one who resists the suggestion that the Joseph narrative belongs in the wisdom literature. See his *Old Testament Wisdom: An Introduction* (Atlanta: John Knox Press, 1981), 40.

10. Crenshaw, *Old Testament Wisdom*, 80.

11. Ibid., 86.

12. Walter J. Harrelson, "Wisdom and Pastoral Theology," *Andover Newton Quarterly* 7 (1966):6–14.

13. Ibid., 11.

14. Richard I. Evans, *Dialogue with Erik Erikson* (New York: Harper & Row, 1967), 111.

15. However, Carol Gilligan has made an important step toward integrating these two theories in her article, "Justice and Responsibility: Thinking About Real Dilemmas of Moral Conflict and Choice," in *Toward Moral and Religious Maturity,* ed. Christiane Brusselmans (Morristown, N. J.: Silver Burdett, 1980), 223–49.

16. Erikson, *Insight and Responsibility,* 222.

17. Capps, *Pastoral Counseling,* 141–44.

18. Crenshaw, *Old Testament Wisdom,* 82.

19. Erikson, *Life Cycle Completed,* 33.

20. Crenshaw, *Old Testament Wisdom,* 56–57.

21. Erikson, "Galilean Sayings," 339.

22. Ibid., 340.

23. Ibid., 351.

24. P. A. H. De Boer, "The Counsellor," in *Wisdom in Israel and in the Ancient Near East,* ed. M. Noth and D. Winton Thomas (Leiden: E. J. Brill, 1955), 69–70.

25. Erikson, "Galilean Sayings," 340–41.

26. Erikson, *Insight and Responsibility,* 49–80.

27. Ibid., 72.

28. Ibid., 75.

29. Crenshaw, *Old Testament Wisdom,* 121.

30. De Boer, "The Counsellor," 56–57.

31. Crenshaw, *Old Testament Wisdom,* 106.

32. Ibid., 125.

33. Capps, "Petitionary Prayer," 140–41.

34. Heije Faber, *Pastoral Care in the Modern Hospital* (Philadelphia: Westminster Press, 1971).

35. David K. Switzer, *Pastor, Preacher, Person* (Nashville: Abingdon, 1979), chap. 1.

36. Erikson, *Insight and Responsibility,* 53.

37. Alastair V. Campbell, *Rediscovering Pastoral Care* (Philadelphia: Westminster Press, 1981), chap. 5.

38. Ibid., 55.

39. Erikson, *Young Man Luther,* 37.

40. Harrelson, "Wisdom and Pastoral Theology," 11.

41. Ibid.

42. Walter Brueggemann, *In Man We Trust* (Richmond: John Knox Press, 1972), 110–11.

43. Ibid.

44. See also Wayne E. Oates, *Pastoral Counseling* (Philadelphia: Westminster Press, 1974), 94.

45. Crenshaw, *Old Testament Wisdom*, 54.

46. J. Coert Rylaarsdam, *Revelation in Jewish Wisdom Literature* (Chicago: University of Chicago Press, 1946), 32–33, 94–95.

47. Erikson, *Life Cycle Completed*, 96–97.

48. Erikson, *Insight and Responsibility*, 96.

49. Erikson, *Toys and Reasons*, 116.

50. Robert Jay Lifton, "Protean Man," *Partisan Review* 35 (1968):13–27.

51. Erikson, *Identity: Youth and Crisis*, 139.

52. Robert Jay Lifton, *The Broken Connection* (New York: Simon & Schuster, 1979), 18–19, and 335–38.

53. See Robert Jay Lifton, *History and Human Survival* (New York: Vintage Books, 1971), chaps. 5–8; *The Life of the Self* (New York: Simon & Schuster, 1976), chap. 5; and *The Broken Connection*, chap. 11.

54. Daniel J. Levinson et al., *The Seasons of a Man's Life* (New York: Alfred A. Knopf, 1978), chaps. 14–15. A fourth mid-life polarity, masculine vs. feminine, does not appear to be relevant to Ecclesiastes.

55. Norman Perrin, *Jesus and the Language of the Kingdom* (Philadelphia: Fortress Press, 1976), 55.

56. Amos N. Wilder, *Jesus' Parables and the War of Myths* (Philadelphia: Fortress Press, 1982), 79.

57. Ibid.

58. Crenshaw develops this skeptical strain in *Old Testament Wisdom*, chap. 8.

59. Perrin, *Language of the Kingdom*, 51–52.

60. Capps, *Pastoral Counseling*, chap. 4.